Best Wishes

Mrs Jean Mc
Chairman

C000061947

Mrs Maureen Bougourd nee Allen
Vice Chairman

Jersey Evacuees
Remember

Best Wishes
From Marian Hougues
14/9/204   nee Elliott

Jersey Evacuees
Remember

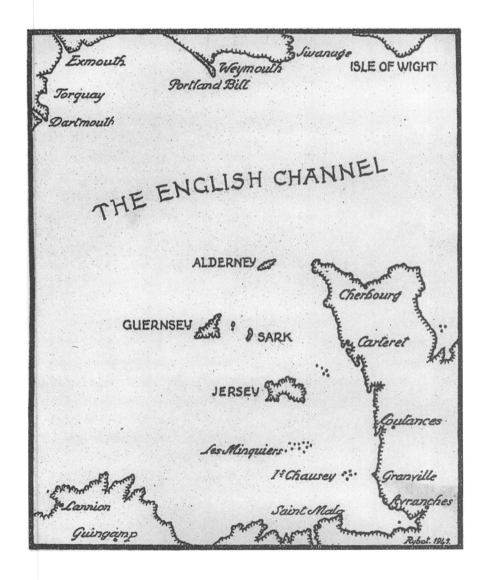

First published by
The Jersey Evacuees Association
in 2011
This edition revised and reprinted in 2012

Edited by Peter Tabb

CHANNEL
ISLAND
PUBLISHING

ISBN 978-1-905095-30-8

www.channelislandpublishing.com

DEDICATION

The Committee and I would like to dedicate this book to our beloved parents, who were very brave and courageous in leaving their island of Jersey, for the benefit and the welfare of their children. To them we are truly grateful that they made such a huge decision. We thank them, love them always, and miss them so very much with all our hearts.

Jean McLaughlin

Jersey Evacuees Association Badge, Created by George Symon.

The Committee. Left to Right: Barbara Carter, Elizabeth Etienne, Maureen Bougourd, Shirley Symons, Jean McLaughlin, George Symons, Robert McLaughlin.

Photograph reproduced by kind permission of Graeme Delanoe

Contents

ACKNOWLEDGEMENTS

The Jersey Evacuees Association gratefully acknowledge with thanks the support of the Sir James Knott Trust in the publishing of this book. It would also like to thank the Jersey Evening Post, Société Jersiaise and all those who granted permission to reproduce their photographs in this book.

Special thanks are due to:
Mr Peter Tabb who gave his time so freely to edit the book
Mr Howard Butlin-Baker (Researcher)
The Constable of St Helier, Mr Simon Crowcroft;
His Excellency the Lt Governor, Lieutenant General Sir Andrew Ridgway, CB, CBE
The Bailiff of Jersey - Mr Michael Birt QC
Société Jersiaise Reference Library for the their invaluable help, especially
Ms Anna Baghiani
Jersey War Tunnels
The Public Library Reference staff
The Jersey Archive Services
The Co-Operative Society and their Helping Hands
Mr Doug Ford – From Jersey Heritage
Mr Rod McLoughlin (Cultural Development Officer)
Mr Chris Addy
Mr Graeme Delanoe
Georgetown Methodist Church
Mrs Jean Cadin for typing various taped interviews
Mrs Elizabeth Etienne for collecting and collating the stories
Chris Stubbs and Simon Watkins of Channel Island Publishing and all who contributed towards the costs of publishing this book.

I would like to thank my dedicated and devoted Committee - George and Shirley Symons, Maureen Bougourd, Barbara Carter and Elizabeth Etienne.

Lastly my love and thanks to my husband Robert, my daughter Karryna Lovesey and my son John James McLaughlin for all their support and encouragement.

Jean McLaughlin
Chairman – Jersey Evacuees Association

9

20th June 1940 and thousands queue at the Town Hall to register for evacuation.

FOREWORD
by Simon Crowcroft

In September 2006 a commemoration was organised by Jean McLaughlin on the Albert Pier which included the unveiling of a plaque to remember the traumatic events of June 1940 when thousands of Islanders had to choose whether to be evacuated to England or to stay in Jersey following its demilitarisation. Jean had discussed the ceremony extensively with me as it was the first time she had organised such an event, and she requested that I wear the scarlet and gold regalia of the Constable of St Helier, together with the chain of office, to heighten the sense of occasion. Although I was unaware of it at the time, one of the Island dignitaries who stood on the quay 66 years earlier, and who tried to persuade people to stay put, was the former Constable of St Helier, John Pinel, the first holder of that office to wear the regalia of the Constableship. Judge Pinel was not the only dignitary who put such pressure on Islanders. In the States' Assembly Jurat Edgar Dorey accused of cowardice those who were thinking of leaving like 'rats and rabbits'.

The wide gap of time between those extraordinarily difficult days in the middle of June 1940 and the present means that the majority of those who are alive to give a first-hand account of the evacuation were children then, and had little or no say in the decision to leave; it was their parents who had to make up their minds whether they would be jumping out of the frying pan into the fire. With the enemy at the gate, as it were, they had no way of telling whether taking refuge in England was a safer option than staying in Jersey, and whether the voyage itself would prove their undoing. It was particularly difficult for mothers whose husbands had already left to join the war effort. The decision to leave would be made, unmade and made again as impassioned family conferences took place across the Island, and evidence of the climate of anxiety and indecision can be seen from the statistics: although 23,000 people registered for evacuation out of the population of 50,000 only 6,600 went through with it. Once they had determined to leave relatives and property behind, they had to join the long queues that formed at the Town Hall for what turned out to be a futile registration exercise, before packing what they could and joining another long queue along the Albert Pier. Even the youngest of their children were aware of their parents' dilemma, and the accounts contained in this book communicate it powerfully down the years, particularly telling details being the thousands of pets that were put to sleep by their departing owners, and the extra layers of clothes that had to be worn when the weather was at its hottest to save precious space in bags and suitcases.

The stories of the evacuees inevitably diverge upon their disembarkation at Weymouth, depending on where they had to live and on the impact that the war had upon them, particularly the bombing raids. However, the experiences of those who returned to Jersey after the Liberation have a common theme in the difficulties of re-integration. Not that this was unique – returning servicemen and women and those who had been interned in Bad Wurzach faced similar challenges – but only a returning evacuee would have been stigmatised for not having endured the Occupation. "At our first assembly, the head mistress made all the children whose parents had 'run away' from the Island stand up in front of everybody." The injustice of this may pale in comparison to the other trials facing Jersey people in the post-war years, but it is thought important enough to record by more than one evacuee whose stories make up this collection.

The members of the Jersey Evacuees Association who have written this book have made a significant contribution to our understanding of the experiences of Jersey people during World War II. Their stories are evocative and moving in themselves, and will also provide a valuable source of material to students of this crucial period in the history of the Island.

Simon Crowcroft,
Connétable of the
Parish of St Helier,
Jersey

INTRODUCTION

After sixty years without recognition and no mention of those who evacuated from the Island immediately before the German occupation I have taken it upon myself to bring us together as the Forgotten Evacuees of Jersey.

We left the Island of Jersey in June 1940 just days before the Germans arrived. The decision to do so was our parents' own and they did so for many different reasons.

Above all it was vitally important to me to find out how many evacuees were still alive and wanted to be acknowledged for the contribution they made to final victory in the Second World War. "Why not?" I asked myself. We were still Jersey people and we just wanted to be accepted back into the community of the Island that we loved so much.

As far as I am aware, no-one has written a book of the experiences of what life was like during those long five years we were at war. The book tells of our experiences and memories of what we saw and lived through as children. We want to convey to everyone reading this book the feelings of what it was like and what we went through, living on the other side of that stretch of water that separates us from England. This book is for all generations to understand the sad and lonely days we endured as children.

In order to compile this book I formed a committee and we collected the memories of those evacuees who were willing to contribute their stories. We raised funds in order to publish the book to make sure that people knew what went on during those long five years of war between 1940 and 1945 while we were away from our beloved island of Jersey.

I feel very privileged and honoured that I had the idea to bring this book about so that today's generations and those following can share our experiences of what we went through. We all thank God that our parents were so loving and caring at a time when we really needed them.

Jean McLaughlin

A REFUGEE'S STORY

Those of you who have had the privilege of visiting Jersey will know much of what there is to know of the beauty of the Island. For others, I will give a brief survey of the little place, where I was born and bred and which had always been to me the loveliest spot on earth.

Lying about 14 miles from the nearest point of France, and about 100 miles from Southampton, and the most distant of the Channel Islands from England, Jersey was naturally in a 'danger area' once the Germans invaded France. But, not dreaming for a moment that French capitulation was likely, we Islanders felt secure from real participation in this war. We knew that the treacherous coastline was in our favour, as far as sea invasion was concerned and also decided that the Islands were far too small and insignificant for the enemy to worry about.

Our militia was mobilizing and many men had crossed to England to join up, voluntarily. Others were waiting the calling up of their age groups. These facts and the shortage of certain foods, etc. were the only signs of war until about June 1940. Then things began looking up. Troops were arriving from England, complete with ammunition, guns and all other gear necessary for the defence of the island. We were told that Jersey was to be made into a "miniature Malta".

This was cheering news because for some days rumours had floated about to the effect that a compulsory evacuation was to be ordered for everyone. Now, however, we felt safe in the knowledge that at any rate we were to be militarily defended.

My husband and I often walked along the piers and seafront and so saw most of the troops arrive. The peaceful atmosphere of Jersey had been shattered; soon we were not allowed near the harbours or on some parts of the Esplanade, but we still had plenty of room to move about and spent our evenings walking along the promenade or sitting on a seat or a sea wall, admiring the beautiful sunsets and the calm blue of the sea in St Aubin's Bay.

It is hard to describe adequately the real beauty of these surroundings. We were facing the sea from the south west of the island. To our left were the cliffs of Fort Regent, beneath these the harbours of St Helier jutted out to sea and not far from the shore, standing out serenely and peacefully from the azure waters was Elizabeth Castle which held so much ancient history beneath its ruins. Then, as one gazed westward, one could see the lovely stretch of sand, running for about three miles to St Aubin, the little village which had been Jersey's first commercial port and behind whose cotils (steep cultivated fields) the sun was setting. With everything so peaceful, it seemed impossible that there could be a war.

The lovely clear sky, the beautiful blue of which was now becoming intermingled with the orange, red and golden hues of sunset and in the sea below, the reflection of all this wonderful maze of colours. Then as time went on the sun became like a huge ball of gold which slowly sank behind the line of trees surmounting the cliffs and at last vanished so that one would expect to be able to run and pick it up from the beach of the bay which rested behind St Aubin.

So another day ended. We would wend our way homewards thanking God for the opportunity we had of seeing the land as He would have it be – always.

On Thursday 13 June I had occasion to go to Gorey, a lovely bay on the south east side of the Island, which faces France and from which, on a clear day, even the buildings on the French coast could be seen.

Continuously during the afternoon we could hear gunfire from France. The villagers said that they could hear that every day so that they often wondered when it would be Jersey's turn.

Then on Tuesday 18 June, during the lunch hour, my husband and I had noticed the troops returning with their gear to the quayside and loading it on to boats. This was mysterious because they had disembarked only the morning before!

However, no-one knew anything but we sensed a certain feeling of unrest in the town and people were talking again – the sort of talk which made you realize at once that 'Dame Rumour' was about. We decided to wait for official news.

Little realising that it would be our last walk for some time; we again spent part of the evening on the West Park seafront, indulging once more in admiration of yet another picturesque sunset. The tide was high and it was such a still evening that the creeping water lapping against the seawall was the only sound to be heard.

Suddenly out of the stillness came a terrific noise of bomb blasts as if the Island itself was being bombed. Some said it was our own airport being blown up, but we discovered later that it was actually St Malo on the coast of France 40 miles to the south of Jersey, that had suffered the bombing at the hands of our own forces.

The next day we received the news of France's capitulation and, of course, realized at once that we were in immediate danger. Gradually the mystery of the returning forces and their gear became clarified – Jersey was being demilitarized. There was to be voluntary evacuation for all who wished to take advantage of it.

We were told to register at the Town Hall if we wished to leave, so as soon as business hours ended I dashed along to enter my husband and my own names.

The arrangement was women and children first, military-aged men next and then the older men. The British Government would supply as many boats as necessary and those who could pay their fare were asked to do so – these would come under Class A. For a few days previously hundreds of people had rushed to the banks to draw out all or most of their money. There was no chance of getting near a bank or the post office that day or the next without queuing for hours. By a lucky chance, we had about five pounds in cash in the house. My firm was able to pay my wages and so we felt able to find the cash for fares.

Therefore I registered as Class A, my husband going on the "military age" list. Nothing was said about tickets; we expected to hear of them the next day. After registering I met my husband and together we went to see my parents whom I had also registered, to save them the bother of queuing for hours. They were out, so I left a note and then we went to our own home. It was only as we entered our little home that the full force of the blow came to us. As we looked around at the familiar furniture and all our hard-earned books, wireless and other precious belongings, that we realized what going away would mean.

We had been too busy during the last few hours to think of all this. Now, the facts hit us hard but still we decided it better to leave. After all, if everything remained all right and the Germans did not invade we could return and if not, if the worst happened, then we should be happier in England without our home, than in Jersey with it. So we reasoned with each other.

It was then 8.00pm and we felt we ought to eat. I arranged a quick meal. As we were eating we wondered how long it would be before we would eat another evening meal in that room. We still wonder!

The half-eaten meal over, packing was the next problem. What should we take? Only 28lbs in weight each! There was no time to be fussy. We had been told that the island would be declared an open town, on Saturday 22 June. This was 19 June. At any moment trouble might commence and then chances of escape would be remote. Previous stories had taught us to realize that procrastination was to be avoided at times like these. So I packed as much clothing as possible into two suitcases and added a few odds and ends to my hats in their box. We decided to wear as much clothing as possible. Of course there were insurance policies and other important papers to pack and all these take up room. Shoes were the heaviest problem and men's suits the largest.

Of our seventy odd wedding presents we were able to pack just three including a small chromium alarm clock, the only heavy gift we could squeeze in. By the time our packing was as complete as it could be, it was 11.30 pm and as we expected a heavy day ahead of us we decided on three or four hours sleep.

It needed no alarm clock to wake us at four o'clock the next morning. People were already astir and we could hear neighbours discussing the situation. Evidently they had not been to bed. By the time we were dressed my husband was wearing three sets of underclothes, a woolen pullover and a suit while I had managed to get into three sets of undies, a frock, a 2 piece serge suit, a tweed coat and mackintosh and hoped to carry a winter's overcoat. Before leaving home we had an apology of a breakfast and I completed our packing. At 6.30am my sister arrived to find out whether we had changed our minds. Standing there among the many things we had to leave behind it would not have been hard to answer "yes" but thank God we had the sense to stick to our decision.

My sister's employer and many of his friends were remaining and had made their staff feel that evacuating would be foolish as everything would be all right.

That sounded sensible when one thought only of what little use our small island would be to the enemy. When, however, one remembered who was driving that enemy – then all the first thoughts of the previous afternoon returned. If for no other reason Hitler would take the Island in order to be able to boast that he had his men on British soil – what a story Herr Goebbels could build around that fact! How the German people would rejoice, in that their Führer had taken the first step towards keeping his promise of invading England by August. So we carried on with the job of looking around our home for any oddments which could be squeezed into our pockets. The maximum weight allowed in luggage per person being only 28 lbs, it might be difficult for the reader to realise just how little that really involved and how one would try to pack only necessary articles. Yet, as I mentioned before, there was not much time for fussing and I have often, since our arrival in England, given way to moments of wishful thinking. "If only I had thought to pack so and so, if only this and that" and so on, but what is the use? It is too late now. Indeed we feel very thankful that we have with us all we have.

Eventually the packing completed and the house attended to as far as was necessary, so that no food was left about to rot or water in kettles to become contaminated, we left to visit my parents.

At 9.00am I reported to the office where I had been employed for twelve years to say goodbye to my employers and colleagues. Most of the staff were leaving and it was a very sad moment for all of us. My husband was at the railway station at that time trying to purchase our boat tickets. We had joined a queue at 8.15am and at 9.30am came away as no-one appeared to be answering queries or likely to open the office.

This was the first sign of muddle. Others followed. We had been told to get information regarding the sailing of the boats from notices on the Town Hall windows. There was a large crowd of people around and when at length we got to the notice board there was nothing on it so we walked along to the Royal Square, alongside the Royal Court House.

Here again we met with crowds but did at length gain some information. Women and children of Class A and military-aged men were to meet at the Weighbridge and embark on the ships in the harbour. Still no information about tickets – the queue had disappeared from the railway office by now but what a waste of time!

Our luggage was at my mother's house, which was halfway between our own house and the harbour. In vain had we searched for a taxi or conveyance of any description. Everything was booked up, probably for carrying the country people to town. Somehow we got along with our cases. It was a terrific struggle for apart from the fact that we were very much over-clothed – it was a typical June day and June in Jersey can be remarkably hot, and was so on this particular day.

All along the streets we passed grief-stricken people, many crying at the state of affairs, others mostly because the animals they loved had just been destroyed for no dog or cat was allowed on the boats. That was of course a sensible arrangement but we could not help but feel sorry for those who had just come from the Vet's office.

So we worked our way in and out of the groups of friends who were questioning the advisability of remaining. Many of the Court officials were telling the people off for leaving. They called it cowardice – but surely it was better for people to leave and work or fight for England, than to remain and be of no use whatsoever to the English Government? Eventually we got to the boat with other Class A folk and military aged men, as instructed by the Bailiff, who was now acting as Lt Governor of Jersey. (The former Governor, being a military man, had left the previous day). Here again we met with a great crowd of would-be refugees. It was now 12.30pm. We stood in that dense mass until 4.00pm being pushed and almost trodden on by many who were getting impatient. Often during those weary hours we wondered whether after all it would not be better to return to our little home. Yet it would have taken longer to get back out of that surging mass than to remain and be pushed toward the gangway to the boat.

When at last our vessel was ready for us to get aboard we heard with horror, the police officers call out "women and children first". It may seem wrong to you who read this, that I should write "with horror", but picture if you can four or five hundred people jammed together like sardines in a tin, with no room to raise a hand, no room to stretch a leg to walk, simply depending on the people behind to push us forward, visualize this and then wonder how we could sort ourselves out into "women and children first". It was a ridiculous state of affairs and in many cases the officials had to let the men who were driven towards the boat get on board first in order to make room for the women.

I decided not to go on board without my husband and so we stood still, along with mothers and babies pushing their way through the crowd. This sudden bit of organization was having the wrong effect. After all the men had been told to join the Class A women and now that the crowd was practically half men it would have been much wiser to let everyone aboard as he or she got to the gangway. In doing that several hours' waiting could have been avoided and much of the discomfort of the crush could have been obliterated. One woman, an American, standing next to me, told her husband she was going back home, but when she looked around and saw what she would have to push her way through, decided to wait.

The first boat was filled by now and the next, a coal boat, drew up at the quayside ready to receive more of this now very tired multitude.

At last we were on board. The next job was to find a comfortable place to sit. Many passengers were already settled on the boards which covered the hold. We eventually made ourselves fairly comfortable on the deck between the side of the ship and the wall of the hold.

As we looked up we realized what a great number of people were above us and as they were very tightly packed together, we hoped very much that they would not be seasick!

Everyone was cheerful by now and a few fellows, who had gone down into the hold, were singing to the accompaniment of mouth organs. There was a huge crowd on the upper pier waving goodbyes. I was pleased no-one had come to see me off. It was bad enough to be leaving. When we had left my mother she had been crying bitterly but I hoped to see her in England in a day or two. She had decided to wait until the older men could leave and come away with Dad.

Looking around the boat however, I saw many middle-aged men. Just another instance of lack of order. I did not blame these men for being there. Since the British Government was willing to supply as many boats as necessary surely it did not matter much in what order the people left? It is a well known ironical fact, in England today, that many women left ahead of their husbands. Before these men could leave the orders issued were "no more men to go". Some officials said that it was disgraceful for this great number of people to be allowed to come into England and inflict so large a burden on the Mother country. What an argument! By breaking up families the authorities were inflicting a far more expensive responsibility on the English councils, for most of the women were now dependent upon Poor-Law aid as their only means of support. Their husbands were on the islands and having a number of children to look after they were unable to seek employment. Others were too old for work. These men could have been doing service or other government work, earning money and probably helping on the War efforts by lending money to the Government and think how many hearts are breaking for lack of news of their loved ones.

I am afraid this tragic situation gains such a hold on me when I think of it, that I wander far from the actual part of the journey of which I should be writing.

You have just read of my surprise at finding middle-aged men on board. I repeat I did not blame them but according to instructions they should have waited on the Island longer. My own father would have been among them had he known that the rules laid down were to be ignored – he was not in England.

Maybe he was among those who were later told they could not leave. One of our men friends, aged only 35, was told that, after he had queued for thirteen hours to register his wife, child and himself. He also was still in Jersey.

Had he gone straight to the ship instead of to register he would, no doubt, have got away. The worst part of this is that no-one on the ship was asked whether he had registered, no word was spoken regarding fares paid; it seemed that all the hours spent at the Town Hall and railway offices had been one long waste of time and energy.

Of course one had to get on to the ship before one realized the utter futility of this queuing up. It was too late then to warn one's people. At about 5.00pm we left harbour. There was promise of a fair trip. Everyone wanted to see the last of the Island and even risked standing until Corbière had been passed. This was indeed a daring feat, for, experienced cross-Channel passengers will know, the sea is usually very rough near that famous lighthouse.

When we had been at sea some time a sailor came on deck carrying a large bowl of 'tea' and a few cups. This was indeed a welcome arrival. Cold water was also offered for those who wanted it. We were all very grateful for these favours.

As night fell we settled down to sleep. The friendliness of strangers was very cheering. Two men next to my husband had a large rug and shared it with us.

Through this kind act we were able to get sufficiently warm to entice sleep. Though this was spasmodic it was very welcome. For the first time since I had donned them, I was thankful for the number of clothes I wore. Night time on the deck of a ship, even in June, can be very cold and this was no exception.

As dawn arrived we bestirred ourselves and tried to make out what part of England we were approaching.

I recognized it at once when I saw a white horse formed on the chalk cliff and felt how very fortunate we had been to get so far along without disaster.

We discovered then that sandwiches and tea were obtainable from below deck. These were very welcome.

All passengers seemed quite bright and chirpy under the circumstances and much laughter could be heard from different parts of the ship.

Not long after this I was looking over the sea when suddenly I saw what resembled a periscope of a submarine. My heart in my mouth I signaled to my husband to look. He too thought we were doomed. I was about to mention this "find" when the ship swung sideways and within a few seconds the 'periscope' was near the rail. It was impossible to make out what it really was, but we breathed a sigh of relief and a prayer of gratitude when we realized our presumption had been incorrect. This was the most eventful moment of the journey for me.

At about 5.30pm we docked at a port. After a long wait and more painful queuing we were certified as fit by a doctor and sent to receive refreshments from the hands of the many kind friends who were giving us their services.

Later we went along to the Customs Office. When we eventually had satisfied the officers that we had no "dutiable" goods we were told to go on our way if we had the money to take us to our destination.

For the first time since 5.00pm the previous day, 20 June, we were free.

With a sigh of relief we left the crowds of evacuees and refugees behind us and stepped out to telegraph our friends of our arrival.

Thus we started our new life. The past had to be forgotten for the time being. The future was to be faced with a strong determination to help wipe out of this world the evil and greed which had taken from us our homes, friends, loved ones and the beautiful Island of our birth.

May God help us to cleanse this wickedness and hatred and so restore to all those things which they have loved long since and lost awhile.

Beautiful Jersey, gem of the sea,
Ever my heart turns in longing to thee
Bright are the memories you waken for me,
Beautiful Jersey, gem of the sea.

From an account written by Mrs Beatrice M. Sainsbury (née Picot)
Source: G.O. Evacuation Escape Box No 1, Société Jersiaise Library

EVENTS LEADING UP TO THE EVACUATION OF THE LT GOVERNOR OF JERSEY AND THE MILITARY GARRISON IN JUNE 1940

On 14 May 1940 the Germans took Rotterdam and the Dutch Government immediately evacuated to London. The very next day Holland capitulated and thousands fled from Paris after reports that the Germans had broken through at Sedan.

On 18 May, Antwerp fell to the Germans and General Erwin Rommel's 7th Panzer Division reached Cambrai on its way to the English Channel coast. A week later the remnants of the Allied armies from Britain, France and Belgium had retreated to Dunkirk and during the following days some 194,000 troops were evacuated with heavy losses sustained particularly amongst the ships (both small and large) taking the troops off the beaches.

By 3 June, 224,686 British and 121,445 French and Belgium troops had been evacuated even though when the Germans entered Dunkirk they took 40,000 French prisoners along with an enormous quantity of vehicles and supplies.

Paris fell to the Germans on 14 June, and the next day the British Government decided that the Islands should be left undefended. A meeting had taken place at the Home Office and Jurat E.A. Dorey attended on behalf of the Channel Islands, returning with the following letter for the Lt Governor. It states:

I am directed by the Secretary of State to say that in the event of your recall it is desired by His Majesty's Government that the Bailiff should discharge the duties of the Lt Governor, which would then be confined to civil duties, and that he should stay at his post and administer the government of the Island to the best of his abilities in the interests of the inhabitants, whether or not he is in a position to receive instructions from His Majesty's Government. The Crown Officers should remain at their posts.

On 19 June, Major General Harrison, the Lt Governor of Jersey, advised the British Government that the Germans were bombarding Cherbourg and if the enemy decided to attack Jersey, he simply did not have enough men or equipment to hold them back. Two days later, Major General Harrison and the garrison left the Island on HMS Philante, with the Bailiff of Jersey taking the Governor's role.

Before he left the Governor said, *"I have been exceedingly happy amongst you all but as you know I have received my orders and duty calls me elsewhere. Goodbye and thank you all for your many kindnesses."*

Sourced from "Occupation Resource '85
Société Jersiaise

THE MEMORIES OF SONIA AHIER-KERR

My name is Sonia Ahier-Kerr. I was born next door to the Town Hall in 1 Parade Place on 14 April 1927.

My father was a book binder and had his workshop at No 5 The Parade. Before the occupation we had three shops and my mother used to look after these as she was the business woman.

Just before the German occupation things shut down and unfortunately we had to leave my mother in Jersey as her mother was too old to leave the Island. In the main I remember the funny things about the occupation. My sister and I 'evacuated' twice. When the war was raging in France everyone was confident the Germans would be stopped at the Maginot line and my mother thought it would be a good idea to evacuate to Brittany of all places! Fortunately we never went there but after a few days the Island started to be evacuated and she decided to evacuate us to Ouaisné where, in those days, we had a bungalow (a beach chalet). My sister, my grandmother and I were taken to the chalet and we were there for three or four days before, one fine morning, my mother appeared again and bundled us back to town and said we are going off to England - you have two hours to get ready and I will try to get some money for you. Everyone was trying to get cash and there were queues at the banks. I had never packed before and being left on my own I did not know what to do. I was about 11years old at the time. I packed some summer dresses as it was lovely summer weather and we were only allowed a small case.

Some clever clogs said we should destroy all our photographs before the Germans came. I didn't think the Germans would worry about photographs of my sister and me on the beach but nevertheless we destroyed our photographs by burning them in the sink so that we didn't set the house on fire. In the meantime our mother arrived with £70 in cash and wisely she sewed it into my sister's corset. Everyone wore corsets in those days. Just as well because when we were on the boat my sister was sick so much that she would have lost a handbag.

Living where we did in the Parade we were almost opposite the Cenotaph where people had gathered and the Bailiff Alexander Coutanche was standing on a chair in front of the Cenotaph, and I remember this very very clearly, he was saying that those people who were being evacuated were "rats leaving a sinking ship".

Anyway, despite his words, we got on this coal boat. Sitting on the deck my poor sister started to be sick almost as soon as we sailed and she did not stop until 16 hours later when we got to Weymouth. One thing that has stuck in my mind clearly as we arrived, cold, tired, dirty and hungry was the Salvation Army dishing out tea and buns on the quay. They were so kind and I always try to support them now. They are wonderful people.

Most evacuees went up north but we were lucky because we had an aunt living in Bournemouth so we found our way there and our poor little auntie wondered why we had come as they had bombs falling in Bournemouth! So telegrams went back and forward and my mother kept saying, "It's all quiet, come home", then, when it became obvious the Germans were going to invade, "No, stay".

We stayed at my aunt's. She had two sons and also two boy evacuees and we two. Her husband was working in Southampton and only came home at weekends. She told us that if we heard a funny noise in the middle of the night it would be the air raid siren and we were to go into her bedroom and get under the bed. We all managed to get under the bed but my poor sister got stuck. We still laugh about her getting stuck under the bed.

Soon we got used to being in England. Unfortunately we had not thought of bringing birth certificates, etc., and as soon as I was old enough I wanted to join the forces, the ATS. My friends joined up quickly but I waited six months because I had to get signed solemn declarations as to my age and by the time I went into the army it was June 1945 and after VE Day.

When VE Day came I was staying with a Jersey family in Bournemouth, their name was Bidois. I do not know their Christian names, it was much more formal in those days, and everyone was Mr or Mrs. We had not known them before but we got to know them. They had two sons Patrick and John Bidois. It was there we heard the wonderful news spoken by Winston Churchill that "Our dear Channel Islands are also to be freed today". We went out and celebrated with cockles and beer.

I went to our church to give thanks and I promised that I would go to church every Liberation Day and I have done so ever since.

When I was in England I went to school until my sister (who was seven years older than me and also my guardian) decided I should go to boarding school in Birkenhead. In Jersey I had been to the FCJ and the Reverend Mother from Jersey had now been transferred to Birkenhead. So I went there but only for a short while, as all the time on the radio they were saying there were bombs falling on Birkenhead! Then it was back to Bournemouth to another school which I did not like very much. I had always been to a Convent school with the Nuns whose teaching is their life, who always helped the children if they had difficulties but this Convent School was staffed by lay teachers and it was a totally different atmosphere. They were just doing a 9-5 job. In something like algebra, if you did not understand, you were always doing corrections but no-one sat you down and explained it properly to you. I remember they were horrified at my Jersey accent and I had special lessons to correct my accent. I would love to get my Jersey accent back.

When the Islands were liberated I got compassionate leave to come home for a while but I stayed in the army for five years and eventually came back here. It was difficult to come back but I love my home. It was emotional to be reunited with my mother who was on her own as my father had died, but she had remarried. We used to get Red Cross letters from my mother and in one she said she had remarried a basket maker from the Basket Works. My sister, in one of her letters, said she was expecting a baby in January having been married for 12 months.

During the occupation my mother kept the shop going and she had two fur coats. She was sorting her coats out one day and felt that one of them was the worse for wear and needed attention, so she took it to Voisins but they said it was not worth repairing. She was going to give it away when her friend suggested she put it in the auction. Apparently the Germans were buying fur coats to send back to their girl friends in Germany. So, my mother put it in the auction and she got £5 for it and some girl friend in Germany got my mother's fur coat.

THE MEMORIES OF MAZEL BAAL née LE SUEUR

It was 3 September 1939 when Germany declared war on Great Britain on a Sunday morning as we were listening to our wireless (now we call it the radio).

I was 20 years of age and engaged, not expecting to marry for another few years, as one did in those days, but my fiancé and others who had previously joined the Jersey Militia were called up and billeted at Fort Regent. In the meantime we decided to marry, as others did, to be able to go away with them, eventually on an open boat (not like today's ships). We got away just days before the Germans took over the Island, eventually arriving at Southampton. When we landed we could only speak to our husbands through barbed wire. I remember my husband giving me his last two pounds then we were told we were going to be billeted up north in Bolton.

It was the first time I had left Jersey. I felt very lost and alone and when one of the wives saw I was on my own she invited me to go with her to her relatives in Farnham, Surrey. We went by train (my first time on a train) but on getting there we realized they could not put us up although they let us stay the night after giving us a hot meal. We slept on the floor for the night. We were so grateful. Next day we went looking for somewhere to stay. Eventually I was taken in by a very nice couple who let me stay with them during the five years of the war, even though I told them I was expecting a baby in six months' time. To my amazement they welcomed me with open arms and I was treated as one of the family. I felt so lucky.

In the meantime my husband's regiment was sent abroad and he was captured in Italy by the Germans and sent to Stalag 4B until the war ended in 1945.

My son and I were able to go back to Jersey in August 1945 and what a welcome we had. We kept in touch with those wonderful friends and once we got our own home together a few years later we invited them over for holidays.

THE EVACUATION
THE BARNETT FAMILY STORY
by Sheelagh Le Cocq

My grandfather, George Edward Barnett, was born in London in 1872. He joined the Army at the age of 14 years and 11 months and by the age of 16 was stationed in India where he fought and won medals on the North West Frontier (Afghanistan). After less than a year back in England he was sent to South Africa to take part in the Boer War, where he was wounded. Once he had recovered he was sent back to England in 1903 and was then posted to the Jersey Militia, D Company. Sergeant-Major Barnett served a further 14 years, mainly at St Lawrence Arsenal, where he was warden. Although his 30 year service ended in 1917 he immediately signed on again for the duration of the First World War, when he was Mentioned in Dispatches.

In 1907 his first wife died and two years later he married the young lady he had engaged to care for his two young children. This lady, my grandmother, Caroline Kate Parker, was born in Worcestershire. They went on to have three children together.

On completion of his Army service he stayed in the Island and in the parish of St Lawrence, where he and his wife ran the village shop.

After the fall of Dunkirk the German Army was approaching the coast and Islanders heard the news that the Channel Islands would not be defended should they invade. When the announcement was made that English born people should evacuate the Island my grandparents realized that it was not advisable to stay – not only were they both English by birth but they thought that my grandfather's Army service would not stand them in good stead with the Germans once they landed. With little time to pack they gathered a few belongings together into the small suitcases that they were permitted to take with them. My mother, who had already been living and working in London, returned to Jersey to help her family evacuate. They arranged with some friends who were remaining in the Island that they would clear their belongings and store them on their farm until such time as they could return and collect them, and that they would hand the keys of their rented house back to the landlord.

The family made their way down to the harbour to get a boat to the mainland, but it was extremely busy and they were forced to wait all day. Eventually an official came around and said that there was no chance of getting away that day, and they were advised to return home and try again the following day.

On returning to the house they had not expected to see again so quickly, if ever, they were horrified to find that it had been broken into and looted. Everything of value had been taken, including a large quantity of silver trophies, engraved cups and salvers which my grandfather had won in shooting competitions, mainly at Bisley. Even my uncles' bicycles had been taken.

The next day they returned to the harbour and managed to get on a boat. On arrival in England my grandmother chose not to go where the officials were sending the Channel Islands evacuees but instead decided to go close to her family in Worcester. Three of her sons joined the Army, the older two serving in the Far East with the "Forgotten Army". My mother, who had returned to England with them, moved from London to Worcester where she worked for the Air Ministry at Hartlebury.

At the end of the war the family could not return to Jersey immediately. My grandfather was terminally ill with cancer and could not be moved, and their youngest son, who was in Germany with the Occupying Forces, was one of the last to be demobbed. The two older boys made the decision to remain in England, one having married an English girl, but after my grandfather died, the family, complete with my mother's husband, returned to the Island. They went back to live in the same parish, but obviously not in the same house. Although many enquiries were made, nothing was ever heard of any of their property which had completely disappeared. It left a very sour taste in their mouth to think that people whom they had probably known and trusted had emptied their house before they had even left the Island. This was one looting which could not be blamed on the Germans, as so many others were.

THE MEMORIES OF MAUREEN BOUGOURD née ALLEN

My name is Maureen Bougourd and my maiden name was Allen, I was born on 16 July, 1939, so I was very young, but my brother, who was nine years older than me, has consolidated some notes.

My brother said it was complete and utter chaos in the way everybody who wanted to go had to queue up at the Town Hall to get their tickets. My father did not want us to be left behind because he wanted to join the Navy which he did, as did one of his brothers, and another uncle joined the Air Force. My Grandma and Granddad came with us, the latter was quite elderly then, but he kept us all together. He was our mainstay, because my father's parents stayed behind in Jersey.

We left in June 1940 although my brother doesn't remember the actual date. We left from the Albert Quay, and he remembers that very well indeed. We left on a coal boat which was called the SS Coral. The boat was for women, children and elderly people only. My father and uncles came to see us off. They were to follow on another boat, which my brother believed to be the last boat to leave. We were on the one before that. In our party was myself, my mother, my brother, Granddad, Grandma and my aunt, my mother's sister, whose husband had joined the Air Force.

According to my brother we were absolutely filthy, covered with coal dust, and so we had to be on top of the boat. For my brother I suppose this was quite an exciting time. I don't remember anything myself. So when my father and uncle were seeing us off, waving us goodbye, little did they anticipate what was to happen next. As the crew was untying the boat, the captain shouted 'Jump aboard, lads!', so they did, leaving with just the clothes they stood up in.

It must have been quite something to do that.

So they came with us. The ship we were on then hove-to somewhere in the Channel until we were joined by two more ships and two British destroyers who escorted us to Southampton. It must have been so difficult, we were not supposed to make a noise because the German submarines might hear us and I was crying. Apparently my brother, who was just 10, sang to me very, very quietly, You are my Sunshine. I often wonder if he meant it, I can't believe he did. Every time that tune comes up, it means a lot.

My father joined the Navy immediately he landed in England and when we arrived at Southampton we were put up at an ice rink where duck boards had been put down to make us more comfortable. That night, and my aunt remembers this quite clearly, there was one of the most terrible air raids on that area, as the Germans bombed the docks. I remember her saying it was really awful. But we moved on quite quickly for the next day we were sent to Wakefield by train, where we were to be stationed. The journey took about four and a half hours.

We were very lucky. My brother always remembers that when we arrived at Wakefield station, the locals' words were, and not in a nasty way at all, 'Oh! They're not black'. I suppose they didn't know where Jersey was and they thought we were going to be coloured people. But they were so warm, so loving, really loving people.

Jersey wasn't on the map then like it is today. He says he will never, ever, forget that. It's a touch of humour and you have to have a touch of humour with something like that. We were taken to Denby Dale Community Centre where we stayed, we think, for two weeks before being allocated accommodation. They really wanted to separate the family. Obviously they were short of places to send people, but my Granddad said he wanted us all to stay together, and we were allocated to a house at 20 Berners Street. We shared the house with the Eckars family and the Greenings family who were from Guernsey. Then, of course, there was us, Mum, Grandma and Granddad and Auntie, who was with us for a short time before she went to Doncaster.

The men from these families joined the Royal Navy, except my uncle who joined the Air Force.

We were given a warm welcome; they were lovely, truly hospitable people. I returned many years later with my husband, and we went back to look at that house. We were standing, looking outside it for quite a while when the door of the next door house opened. A lady emerged, wearing a cross-over pinny, a good old Yorkshire woman, and her name was Mrs Musgrove. I never will forget her. She looked at me and she said after all those years, 'You're Maureen Allen. Come here I want to give you a big kiss'. We went in, she gave us a cup of tea, and sat back in her rocking chair, it was unbelievable.

That's going back a bit now, say about 30 years ago, but a long time after the war. She remembered the family and everything about us. It is amazing; she was such a warm, loving person. They were lovely warm people the way they accepted us into their houses.

My brother and I went to St Mary's School, but being older he then went on to the Cathedral Boys Secondary School. It was three miles away and he had to walk. In the winter he almost disappeared in the snow and we only had clogs on our poor feet. That's why I don't like snow. It was the first experience of snow for both of us. Despite all the upset, they made us very welcome. We had the Jersey and the Guernsey Group Organisation. They used to give tea parties, and even the Mayor gave us a tea party.

With Dad away on the Russian convoys, we didn't see him very often. My most vivid memories were of those awful sirens. Even during the day when they tested them, they were horrendous. Another thing was the German bombers; when we heard their noise in the daytime, which was unusual, we all had to get into the school as quickly as we could. Afterwards the siren sounded, and even though I was very young that noise has stayed with me forever.

Every night was horrendous. They took us down to the cellars most nights, but occasionally to a brick-built shed in the back garden, which was horrible.

I suppose we didn't know any better but even as child, I would think, not again! It happened very frequently since it was not that far from London, really. Also that dreaded doodlebug was an awful thing. The sudden silence of it, and even now in my head I can visualise it, then the fire brigade coming clanging along. It is a memory that sticks with a child.

We had good times, but we had those horrid times as well. One of the horrid things was having to carry my Mickey Mouse gas mask with me all the time, which I hated. A good memory was waking up one Christmas morning to find Father Christmas had left me a wooden wheelbarrow. Only later did I discover that Granddad had sawn up the family's one and only clothes horse to make this wonderful barrow. Oh, he must have been in trouble!

To our parents it must have been terrible and I don't know how they coped really. My Mum had her mother and father so she was in a better position than most people. She had the reassurance of her own parents being there.

It was very difficult because I used to think to myself, who is this man who would arrive every six months or so, and throw a little stone up at the window? It was my father in his sailor's uniform. I always remember I used to feel I loved that man, but wondered who he was. I didn't realise he was my father, and although I thought he was lovely, it was a very strange feeling.

My Dad served on HMSs Intrepid and Zephyr. HMS Intrepid was sunk and he went down with it, but he survived. He was lucky but when he came back his health had suffered. When he got back, he worked at anything he could. He didn't worry what he did, because it was difficult to get work and to keep your home together again. They had absolutely nothing at all and that must have been the worst part of it.

My father was quite a character. He was lovely, but we didn't have much time to spend together. Little did I know what my father had gone through mentally on those Russian convoys and I'm proud of what he did for his country and his Island. He was demobbed about eighteen months after the end of the war. I think sometimes that what they did has been forgotten, which is sad. I had wonderful parents and grandparents and heaven knows how hard it was for them.

We stayed over there for a bit at the end of the war, while the family decided what they wanted to do. Eventually they all wanted to come back to Jersey, which we did at Christmas 1945. Unfortunately my grandfather had died in Wakefield during the war. I should think he would have been in his late fifties and he died of cancer of the throat. I can still remember my dear Granddad used to knit our socks, little socks, to keep our feet warm. He had been a military man himself, in the army and in India for many years.

On our return to Jersey I went to Halkett Place School, while my brother went to New Street School. It was not an easy time at first as I was made to feel different to the other children who had stayed behind in Jersey. I could not understand why they called me and my family cruel names, but later on I realised it was because we had left the Island in 1940.

Right through the war in his sailor's cap my father kept a wartime prayer and a photograph of me. Although he was torpedoed twice (once with the loss of a destroyer) the prayer, the photograph and the hat and my father survived.

These reminiscences are taken from an interview conducted with Maureen by Jersey War Tunnels.

A friend of Maureen's uncle who was in the RAF with him, painted this picture for the Evacuees who had moved to Wakefield.

It hung on the wall where they held social meetings for both Jersey and Guernsey Evacuees. This picture is still as new and was shown at Georgetown Methodist when Maureen gave her talk on her experiences

Standing at back Maureen's parents Mr and Mrs C. F. Allen;
seated Maureen's grandparents Mr and Mrs Lobb, with Maureen and her
brother in the centre

Maureen Allen

THE MEMORIES OF BARBARA CARTER
née Houguez

My name is Barbara Carter and I was born on 18 November 1936. I had a brother "Sonny" who was five when we evacuated, while my eldest sister Natalie Jean was six years old. My new baby sister Ann was only born on 28 April 1940, making her the youngest baby to leave Jersey. Our parents were Reginald and Natalie (née Diment).

My mother was so young; she got married at 17 and had had three children by the time she was 20. The youngsters today complain but my goodness how those girls survived, I don't know. By the time Mum was 24 she had the responsibility of four young children and Dad was away. That's when you look back and think!

Obviously, just coming up to four years old when we left Jersey, I don't remember a great deal. I only remember the hustle and bustle and worry and upset for my parents of taking four small children across to England. I don't think that we children understood what was happening to us, but I do remember my mother only having one small case and most of that was filled with nappies for a six-week old baby. We had, more or less, the clothes we stood up in.

We were a group of nineteen, I think it was, from our family, actually travelling together, so my mother had quite a lot of help with the four children because my aunts, were still teenagers, could help. My grandmother was with us as my grandfather was in the Navy, and he was already in England.

We were on one of the last boats to leave the island. My aunt who queued up to get tickets or passes for us and was turned back at the last minute. She went again the following morning and waited about eight hours before she finally managed to get passes for all the family to go.

When we arrived in England, the Salvation Army were there to hand out milk for the babies and food for the children. We were taken to a rest centre. I don't remember much about that but I think there was a lot of excitement. From there we were allocated to different parts of the country.

We went on to Bolton and on arrival went again to a Salvation Army refuge or a municipal building, maybe the Town Hall. We went on to several different places and then we were allocated to houses. We shared with another Jersey family, and that lady's name was Roselle Le Louarn; she had three children and they had the top floor of a big Victorian house, while we had the bottom floor. It worked out beautifully because they both looked after each other's children, and would take both families to school.

I can remember great parties - when I say parties I mean bread and jam – when there were seven children in the great big kitchen, which we all shared.   There were not enough ingredients to make a birthday cake, so it was really make believe and pretend to make it into something for the children. I remember once my mother said to Mrs. Le Louarn that she would go out and queue as they had heard of some oranges in town. I don't think I will ever forget that as long as I live. It's something I tell the children when I visit the schools. She came back with one great big Jaffa orange which was all she could get. She cut it into quarters for each of us and we sucked on that quarter of an orange all afternoon.

Food wasn't plentiful but, goodness, weren't our mothers resourceful ! They got whatever they could get for us, and we never really went without.

My mother, who died in 2003, stayed friendly with Roselle all her life, and she only died in 2009.

For me the years spent in that house were happy times although in the background there was the constant sound of the sirens. We were terrified, I can remember my mother had the use of the cellar and she used to drag mattresses down there so that we children would be safe. Nevertheless that was a worry to my mother because of the dampness in the house which did not have adequate heating and, of course, we were having to go underground so often. It was nearly every night that we were down there, with the sirens constantly sounding and bombs going off.

The house was quite near to the docks, and although the bombs didn't actually hit Bolton they were dropping quite close. As children you just remember the noise.

I remember all the railings round the schools and the houses were taken down because they were needed for the war effort.

Unfortunately, I contracted tuberculosis while I was in Bolton, so I spent quite a lot of time in hospital. At first they started me off with treatment which wasn't effective. They then took a gland out which left me with a great big lump and I couldn't turn my head. But they had to find out where the TB had come from for, as you know, it can run in families. They did find out, just before we came back to Jersey, that it had come from the milk of cows infected with tuberculosis. Quite a few people were infected by untested tuberculin cows.

After I had the operation, I went to a convalescent home out in the country. Bolton was a damp place anyway, and this new place was like a glass house, which they thought would be helpful for my condition. I was there for about six weeks and I just recall it was in the country. I also used to have ultraviolet treatment at Bolton General Hospital, which is still there. I can still remember the smell.

There were several children and first of all we started off lying on the beds. We wore goggles and the ultraviolet light was shone on us, ten minutes on your back and ten minutes on your tummy. As we got better, we could sit round on chairs in a circle and a great big light shone all around us. I was very, very weak and fragile and my Mum asked what should she do with me when she got me back home. They said once I got back to the Jersey sunshine I would be fine – and I was. I made a full recovery.

Some of our relations lived close to us and we used to go on a tram to visit my grandmother. Her daughters still lived with her and eventually they married Bolton boys. We were still visiting Bolton until three years ago when my uncle who lived in Bolton died. My three aunts all worked in the cotton mills. One of them worked in the Anchor factory where they made coloured threads for embroidery and another one worked in an ordinary cotton factory. My other aunt, who had had a good job in Jersey at either Voisin's or De Gruchy's, went into a department store in Bolton. They went to a dancing school in the evenings which, I think, was to relieve the boredom. They went on to become quite good dancers and had their own schools for teaching - a bit of light relief.

Mr Le Louarn, our neighbour, worked in the mines and my father went into the army, he was asked if he wanted to go into the mines or join the forces. He wasn't a very strong person, he was only a little man and there was no way he was going to go into the mines, so he went into the forces. Before he joined up, he worked in the De Havilland factory and he was also an ARP warden, going out at night to patrol the streets. I think I may still have his black band with red ARP across it. He went into the army. Because he wasn't passed A1 (he wasn't that fit) he used to drive DUKWs.

I don't quite know where he was, but I know he was also in the cookhouse even though he was a terrible cook. When he came back and my mother had her last baby after the war, Dad was doing the cooking and I can remember it was horrendous. However did he get to work in the cookhouse! I suppose they thought 'got to give him something to do'. But as I said he was originally driving DUKWs and he used to tell us about it. It was always a great occasion when he came home on leave.

While we were away birthdays and Christmases were what our parents made for us. There were never really any presents, I think we were given a couple of pairs of socks or something like that, which my mother had probably managed to buy for a present. I don't think we expected anything, we didn't know any better and we thought a couple of pairs of socks were wonderful.

All the clothing we had was 'hand me downs', presumably from the Salvation Army, because we didn't have more than just one change of clothes, and that was all.

This is a bizarre story.

I had a friend, her name was Anne and we lived on this side of the road and she lived on the other. Her father was a policeman and her mother was the tiniest little lady you ever saw. I think they felt sorry for we evacuees, so I used to get quite a lot of clothes from this friend, who was the same age but a little bit bigger than me. I used to spend a lot of time with her family and I can still remember her mother making bread and leaving it to rise with a cloth on the top.

I lost touch with her once we came back to the Island;   she obviously married and I married and we lost contact. Last year in August, I got a phone call and a voice said "Are you Barbara Houguez who was a little evacuee?" I said "Yes" and she replied "You might not remember me, but I am Anne Crofton, your best friend from all those years ago." She had come to Jersey for the first time ever for her 50th wedding anniversary. She was with her husband, and she had said to herself 'In Jersey I had an evacuee friend'. She remembered I had a brother and looked him up in the telephone directory, R. Houguez, and spoke to Marion. Marion told her I was her sister-in-law and gave her my number. I told her I couldn't believe it as I had been talking about her to my children only six weeks previously. My daughter had said to me if only I had the name I could go on Facebook and get in touch with her.

Anyway, we met up, she was staying at the Lyndhurst Guest House, about two minutes away from where my daughter lives. My daughter and I joined her and her husband, and I couldn't believe that she knew me straight away. It was the last day of their holiday, and she said she wished she had got in touch sooner. We went out for the day and we are now in touch.

The funny thing is she married a 'John' and I married a 'John'. She has four children, and I have four children, she has three sons and a daughter, and I have three sons and a daughter. Her daughter is called Jo-Anne, hyphenated because of her husband being John and she being Anne. I had a late daughter after a 15 year gap and she has the same name with exactly the same name connection. She married a J.C. Cook, and I married a J.C. Carter. How bizarre is that? We couldn't believe the similarities we came across. So that was the story. I think it was about a week before we had our 'do' down at the Hotel Ambassadeur, and I just wish I could have taken her to that dinner. It has been 60 odd years, quite incredible.

I was very happy at school. I went to a lovely school when I was five and a half. My mother used to walk us to school and my brother Sonny used to run back as soon as she had left to go home again. Then she had to go all the way back to the school again. I think the other children teased us because of our accents but generally we fitted in.

We also went to Sunday School which was a nice experience mixing with a lot of other children. What I don't actually remember is any other evacuees in our area since all the others were children from Bolton. They were all OK and we had lots of little parties at Sunday School. Each one would be a big occasion and we would perhaps get a couple of sweets each.

We had coupons and when Mum could afford it she would buy sweets. About once a fortnight, my mother would give us a little coupon cut out of the ration book for two ounces of Dolly Mixture or something like that or even a small Fry's chocolate bar. The kids, of course, can have sweets every day now, which isn't good for them. The Americans were very generous about giving out sweets.

Sports Day was always a great occasion at the school. At the bottom of our road there was Bolton Boys' School, which was a special selective school for the bright boys. I can remember the archways to get into the school. The first time I was selected to go to a Sports Day, I was just nine years old and my mother had to beg, borrow and steal clothes for me to take part in the running race as we had to wear white clothes.

Going down to the boys' school was desperately important and, apart from that, I was just feeling so special. It was just everyday running, but Sports Day was a very special day.

Another recollection was my mother taking us for walks and just getting us out of the house was quite something.

One incident I don't think I'll ever forget, happened at a place called Rivington Pike, which was quite famous in Bolton. She had walked us what seemed miles and miles to this area and we sat on the grass having a picnic of bread and jam. All of a sudden this drove of horses came galloping towards us and I don't think anybody has ever seen anything move so fast, they were literally coming straight at us. I can't remember what the event was called, but it was a special thing. Up till practically the day she died, my mother still spoke about this drove of horses and how she thought we were all going to be killed. That was another great day in the history of our outings. Outings were usually to the park, there were two parks near there, with swings, or just going out for walks.

When it came the time to return to Jersey, we didn't all go back together. Some of the girls had got married and stayed in Bolton. Auntie Joan came back, Auntie Betty came back, so my grandmother stayed behind with two of them, who were working at the time. One of them then returned to Bolton and married and lived there. So when we came back there was just my mother with the four children as my father was still in the Army and stayed in England until he was demobbed in 1947.

We came back to Jersey in September 1945.

From Bolton we were taken to a rest centre in London where we stayed there for two nights. Then we went by train down to Weymouth where we were put on an overnight mailboat and I was as sick as could be. Apart from that it was uneventful.

We were met by a jubilant Jersey family. They were all my father's family and had arranged a home for us because all Mum and Dad's furniture had gone into storage in my grandfather's loft in St Martin. They managed to find a nice little house in St Martin called Winkleigh. Mind you it had only one and a half bedrooms and two rooms downstairs. When my father was demobbed, Mum and Dad slept downstairs, and the three girls slept in one bedroom. There was only my one brother Sonny and he slept in the little box room. The toilet was a long way up the garden, which to us was totally alien, as we had been used to a bathroom and flush toilets in Bolton.

Once back to live in Jersey, my mother had to go up the garden and boil the clothes in a great big copper. We had probably gone from bad to worse, it was horrific, but at the same time it was lovely to come back to nice clean fresh air.

Soon we were housed by the Housing Committee who had built some brand new accommodation at St Martin's Arsenal. By then my younger brother Barry had been born and for about three years they housed us there in a brand new property, until my grandfather died.

My Dad managed to buy my grandfather's house and we lived in St Martin for many years and at heart I am a St Martin's girl – and I always will be.

When we returned to Jersey we got a bit of teasing from other kids, who called us 'rats' and all the rest of it, for having left Jersey. I can remember my mother said, and I don't know whether it's true or not, that because my grandfather was in the Navy and my mother was born in England (my grandmother was visiting him at the time), they said my mother was English. Had we stayed in Jersey, we might have been sent to a German prisoner of war camp and obviously my father didn't wish that to happen. So that was one of the reasons why we went to England .

My links with the Jersey Evacuees Association and speaking with other evacuees, has strengthened my recollections of that time. Schools are now asking evacuees to talk to them about their experiences. My daughter is a school teacher and so far I have been to seven different schools and told my story and the children are absolutely enthralled. They love it and the letters I have had back, thanking me for going and explaining what happened to us, really are amazing.

There are a lot of things I do not remember but there were monthly newsletters printed, some of which can be seen at the Public Library, and one of them mentions the Houguez family. There are not many people called Houguez left in Jersey, and those that are here are all related and the name could die out this century.

These reminiscences are taken from an interview conducted with Barbara by Jersey War Tunnels.

THE EVACUATION MEMORIES OF PAT DUBRAS née BURTON

I was born in Jersey in September 1932 and had a brother, Roger, born in 1936. My parents were both born in England and met on the boat bringing them to Jersey. My mother, Hilda Miller, always known as Toni, was a hairdresser and actually worked in the Dubras Hairdressing Salon when she first came to the Island. My father, Leslie Burton, was a professional ballroom dancing teacher, teaching and demonstrating with my mother at West Park Pavillion.

When war was declared, my mother had a salon called Maison Burton in Charing Cross and we lived in the three storey flat above. My father went to England to join up, but was turned down because of his bad eyesight. When he heard of the rumours about the Germans occupying Jersey, he jumped on one of the last boats coming over to take back the evacuees.

My mother, who had decided not to leave the Island, was doing a perm in the salon when my father burst in to tell her she must leave. They argued for ages but eventually my father persuaded her that they must go, because of the two children.

They queued for hours through the night in Gloucester Street to get tickets on one of the last boats. They were told they could only take two suitcases between the four of us. We left our young dog, Tinker, in the care of the girl who looked after us during the day, while Mum was at work, and got into the car. I was carrying two dolls, a white one called Toddles, and a black one called Nina, and my brother had a fluffy dog called Sixpence. These were the only personal possessions we were to own for a long time.

My father drove down to the harbour and. abandoned the car as we had no other place to put it! We boarded the boat which was packed, and spent a cold night sitting on deck, leaning against the funnel, and arrived in Weymouth. We stayed one night in a large room in a hotel, which was the first time my brother and I had been away! The next day, Mum, my brother and I went to stay with our grandparents in Portslade, Sussex, while my father tried to find accommodation near the munitions factory he was now working in, near Woolston, Southampton.

They rented a little house just down the road from the banks of the Solent. We had no clothes, no furniture and no money. There was an Anderson

44

Shelter in the back garden, but it had flooded, as a German bomb had hit a water main. We had a munitions factory just down the road and five huge oil containers at the end of the garden; little did we know we were to be sitting targets for the German bombers!

My brother and I never slept in a bed for the whole of the war. We were put to bed on a mattress under the stairs and when the Germans came over every night at 11.00 pm the sirens went, and our parents picked us up and carried us up the road to the pub, where we slept on the floor of the cellar until the All Clear was sounded. As they ran, I can remember the sky all lit up by searchlights shining on huge barrage balloons. Later on in the war we could hear the noise of doodlebugs passing over and dreaded the noise stopping since that meant they were plunging to earth.

I could not go to the local school as it was full, and my mother had no means of getting me in anywhere else. I spent the day wandering along the shore of the Solent collecting shrapnel. I had a huge tin of it and, of course, didn't realise it had come down the night before red hot! After a year, my father was moved to a factory in Romsey, so we moved to Chandlers Ford, just outside Eastleigh. My mother found a lady called Mrs Simmons prepared to take us in to share her ground floor flat of a large old house. Her husband was in the RAF and she had two daughters and a mother, who occupied a room, with a smelly pekinese and a monkey with rickets which sat on a perch in her bedroom all day. My parents and brother slept in Mrs Simmons' dining room and I slept in the hall on a make shift camp bed. It was freezing cold and every one walked past my bed!

I was very lucky that before we left Jersey I had been taught to read by Mr and Mrs Harmon who ran the St Helier Girls School in Stopford Road, but I hadn't been to school since and I was now aged nine. My mother heard of two teachers who had been bombed out of a Convent in Southampton who were conducting lessons in the lounge of a private house of one of the mothers of a pupil from the Convent. I went there by bus and there were about nine of us squeezed into one room sitting at makeshift tables. We were all different ages and standards, and had no idea what we should be doing! Miss Watts gave me a mauve Maths book which I didn't understand. I was told to solve the problems, so with the answers at the end of the book, I had to work out how to do them. Miss Adams was an incredible English teacher who taught me how to write properly, good spelling and how to speak well.

She also taught me elocution, and I would stand and say my poems to her in the downstairs cloakroom, which was the only private place! She even entered me in an Eisteddfod in Bournemouth and Mum took me there by train, a great excitement. Unfortunately, while eating our sandwiches in a park at lunch time, I slipped in the paddling pool, and got soaking wet! We managed to dry the back of my skirt, but I had to recite "The Silver Birch is a Dainty Lady" with no knickers on!

When I was nearly eleven we moved to Eastleigh, where my parents rented a house near the railway. It had no furniture at all, so Roger and I slept inside the Morrison shelter which was the only thing in the lounge. It was a huge iron construction with a solid top and mesh all round the sides. Most uncomfortable it was, too. My father made a table out of bits of wood and we sat on orange boxes but the house had a garden, which was marvellous, not only for we children but my mother loved having somewhere to hang the washing. She also tried her hand at growing vegetables.

There was a school just up the road called Eastleigh County High School and my mother went to the headmaster and pleaded with him to take me in.. He must have taken pity on my mother as he set me some sort of Exam, which I managed to pass. I found myself in a big school for the first time in my life, tackling subjects like science, geography and history and learning to play hockey and rounders – games that I had never heard of. I was always an avid reader and soon discovered the public library which proved a godsend to me. I couldn't believe I could just walk in there and take books away with me.

It was a long walk into Eastleigh, and I only owned one pair of shoes which had been sent by the Red Cross from America by a boy called Billy Eldred. I did try to keep up a pen friend relationship, but we didn't have much in common. What's more the shoes were too small and agony to walk in. They were black lace-ups and I hated them, but it was no use saying anything. My mother found a part time job at a hairdresser's in Eastleigh, which at least helped with a bit of money. Then, in 1943 she found she was pregnant with my sister, and was very upset. She didn't believe it at first, just complained of a bad back! She kept on working till just before the birth, cycling to the salon in an old tweed coat strained round her. I can remember being so embarrassed, at twelve, at having a pregnant mother that I would ask her to meet me down the road and not outside the school!

Margot was born on 13 June 1944 while my father was out on his motorbike delivering despatches for the Home Guard. Somehow, life continued, till I came home from school one day, and saw my father's haversack on the kitchen table, covered in blood and with his enamel mug tied to it, squashed flat.

He had been knocked off his motorbike by a car, and was in hospital fighting for his life, with all the bones down one side of his body broken. I had no idea what had happened until my mother came home much later to tell us. Mum went every day to the hospital in Southampton, while I stayed home at the age of 12 to look after my baby sister... Our father gradually recovered but had a permanently bent left arm and a bad limp. He was never able to dance or work again.

We all carried on till the end of the war. I do not know how Mum managed or what we lived on.

I do remember my first kiss, a peck on the cheek from a boy called Donald Miller. He was wearing short trousers and black lace up boots and chased me down the road playing 'Kiss Chase' and waving his arms like a windmill!

I clearly remember the end of the war, with all the celebrations, the street party with trestle tables the length of the road, covered with food I had never seen before, flags, balloons and such joy and good nature from everyone.

We were unable to go back to Jersey at once as my parents couldn't afford the fare but my mother went back in November 1945 to see what was left of our home. Unfortunately, it was just at the time I was getting confirmed, so Mum couldn't be there. She had made, by hand, a brown and orange check Viyella dress for me, but of course, when I got to the church, all the other girls were in white!

Somehow we returned to Jersey in 1946 and went back to our house in Charing Cross. There was nothing left; the Germans had moved in there for a while and local people had cleared the house of anything useful. The only interesting thing we found, right at the top of the house, was the life-size doll that my father used to strap to his feet, to demonstrate his ballroom dancing. I often wondered what the Germans thought about the lady in blue velvet in the room upstairs!

My mother was left with bills that had been run up by someone who had run the hairdressing salon until stocks had run out. She started all over again to get the business up and running.

I started at the Intermediate School in Brighton Road and there were a few other pupils who had been evacuees, now returned to the Island and four of the girls became very good friends, and were known as 'the terrible four'. I managed to be sent out of most German lessons as I refused to learn German under any circumstances!

At our first assembly, the head mistress made all the children whose parents had 'run away' from the Island stand up in front of everybody. We were mortified, and so embarrassed because, of course, everybody knew each other and everything was very strange.

After a year, the States decreed that my 'scholarship' allowed me to go to the Girls College, so I started again. Luckily the four girls all came too, but I was in a higher form due to my birthday being in September. All the girls in my form looked like young goddesses to me, talking about their horses, tennis, swimming and, of course, boys!

There were good things too. Thanks to a marvellous English Teacher called Miss Webb I discovered drama and for the first time I appeared on the stage which I loved! I managed to scrape through my School Certificate despite spending a lot of time playing table tennis in the Sixth form Common Room!

Things were very tough as we had no money and my father was always too ill to work and I was never able to ask any friends home. My mother worked every moment to provide for us all, and my father eventually died of cancer when I was sixteen, Roger twelve and Margot four. Mum kept on working and managed to buy the property but unfortunately it was requisitioned by the States. They had plans to put a larger road through Dumaresq Street so she was forced to move out. Nevertheless she actually found a new job as warden in a house let to girls from the United Kingdom working in a bank. Somehow she seemed to be able to remain cheerful despite a very hard life.

Undoubtedly the war robbed us all of any sort normal childhood, and in the aftermath my teenage years were very difficult. The only good thing is that since my parents were both born in England, had we stayed it was very likely we would all have been deported to Germany, and goodness knows what might have happened.

Let us all hope our children will never know such hardships.

THE MEMORIES OF MARIAN HOUGUEZ née Elliot

I am Marian Houguez (née Elliot) and I was born on 10 October 1938. My parents were William and Rosalie Elliot, and in June 1940 I was 15 months old and my brother Ron was thirteen years older than me when we all left Jersey on a coal boat, sailing through the minefields and, after being helped by the Salvation Army, eventually ended up, like a lot of other evacuees from Jersey, in Bolton, Lancashire.

As I was only 15 months old, I haven't got many memories, except for the noise of gunfire, planes passing overhead and sirens wailing. However, I do remember going to St Bartholomew's School in Bolton, but not a lot about it.

We were put up in a nice house with cotton factories behind it and my father worked in an ebony factory. I don't know what he did there but he also used to go out on ARP duties which meant that my mother and I often had to go to air raid shelters on our own whenever there were raids going on.

Unfortunately, my father became ill and contracted tuberculosis.

By coincidence my husband Reg with his parents, Natalie and Reg Houguez, and his sisters Jean, Barbara and Anne, also left Jersey the same way and we all ended up in the same place together. They had another son, Barry, when they got back to Jersey. Reg Houguez, my father-in-law, died on 28 November 28 1978 and his widow Natalie died on 24 August 2002.

I cannot remember the year we came back to Jersey but we were put up in the Chelsea Hotel, later moving to Winchester House in Winchester Street. It was there, when I was seven years old, that I found my father lying on the stairs and he died very shortly afterwards because of the TB he had contacted in Bolton. My brother Ron died in 2008.

Back in Jersey I worked at the Summerland Knitwear Factory. I worked there for quite a while where a person called Jean was teaching me my job. We got talking and it turned out that both our parents had come across each other in Lancashire, so naturally we asked our parents what had happened.

After speaking, we found out that they went on the same coal boat, stayed in the same school and we had all slept in the same beds together. After that we were all found individual places to live, but it has all turned out to be quite a laugh.

49

I was with my husband for years when I was tiny, and had actually been sleeping in the same bed!

I then went out with Jean's brother, Reg. I was 16 years old and 4 years later we got married. We had two daughters, Deborah and Beverley, and we celebrated our Golden Wedding on 15 August 2009.

We were together as evacuees when we were very young, we met up again eventually and got married and you could say that the Salvation Army was responsible!

What a coincidence that we should be on that same boat and that I should work at a factory which led me to meeting Reg again.

These reminiscences are taken from an interview conducted with Marian by Jersey War Tunnels.

THE MEMORIES OF NATALIE JEANNE née Houguez

My name is Natalie Jean Jeanne, née Houguez, and I was born on 18 October 1934.

My mother was one of nine children, so we were a large family, and we decided, as a family, to evacuate to England. Four uncles were already in the Army and my grandfather had already been called up to serve in his second world war, in the Navy.

We held a family meeting to see if we should stay or go and it was decided we would leave. Being parents of four young children, myself the eldest, and three others, they decided we would go as well. We were only able to take one suitcase per family which was mostly baby clothes for my young sisters so we actually only had the clothes we were wearing and no other belongings at all. The children all had labels on their coats with their names on.

We did not own our own house in Jersey but rented a small cottage at Sion so we had to leave everything. After we had gone my father's family, who were staying, came and cleared the cottage and put things into their loft. Naturally when we came back there were quite a few things missing which was only to be expected if they ran short of things. When we came back we were unable to have that cottage as there was someone else living in it so they found us three rooms at St Martin. We had left Jersey on Thursday 20 June 1940 which was the day after the Island was demilitarised. The Germans invaded on Monday 1 July 1940.

My aunt told me that the morning before we left Jersey she had to take their dog to the Animal Shelter and it was a terrible sight that met her eyes. A long queue of people with dogs, cats, rabbits, etc. was all waiting to have them put to sleep as they were leaving Jersey and could not take their pets with them.

We left the Island on a coal boat and travelled in the hold. There were quite a few other family members on the boat as well. There were about fourteen in our family group, grandmother, five aunts, an uncle and a cousin. There was one aunt there with two children who decided at the last minute that she did not want to go saying she would go on the next boat but, as it turned out this was the last boat , which had just delivered coal to the Island, so when we arrived on the mainland it was a strange cargo that got off; babies, children and adults covered in coal dust!

As we crossed the Channel there were planes flying overhead but we were told not to be frightened as they were escorting us. I was only five and a half at the time and I can only remember certain things. I have asked questions to refresh my memory but unfortunately I have lost my mother and father and most members of the family are no longer with us. There are only two members of my mother's family left, one an aunt of 91 and the other about 79 but unfortunately she has dementia so I cannot ask her anything.

When we arrived in England we had to go by train up to London and from there up to the north of England. When we got to Bolton, Lancashire, we were put in the Municipal Hall until they could find somewhere for us to live. The authorities and people were marvellous to us in Bolton and I think we should be eternally grateful for them seeing we were all taken care of through the war years.

When we eventually arrived in Bolton, my father went to work in the De Havilland aircraft factory at Lostock and in the night-time he worked in the Civil Defence and had to go out in his tin hat and gear. Towards the end of the war he was called up and I remember my mother was very upset and crying and so were we children but he was sent to train in the RASC and he ended up driving DUKWs and they sent him down to Yeovil but he was so sick on the DUKWs that they put him in the cookhouse where he was making buckets of porridge and tea for the soldiers, so he wasn't on active service. One of my uncles in the army went missing on active service a few times but, thank God, he always came back safe and uninjured to my aunt and cousin.

When we left Jersey I had not started school as I was just five and a half and in Jersey at that time you did not start school until you were six years old but as soon as I got to England I had to go to school. We had to go with a shoe-bag on our backs and our gas masks and if there was a raid and the sirens went off during school time we had to go into the shelter at the school.

We went to live at 17 Shrewsbury Road, Bolton, which is still there today as is my school friend, who now lives in Bury. She has been a friend since I was five and a half and we are still friends, going backwards and forwards to each other, writing letters and making trunk calls. We have never been out of touch with each other. She sent me photographs of the house we lived in. While we were there they had removed the railings which had to go to be melted down to make weapons and things. When my friend went to take photographs of the house she knocked on the door and spoke to the people who live there now, telling them that during the war two families from Jersey had lived there. They were very interested to learn about this as they had no idea.

My mother and father had the downstairs front room to live in and in the back room were another family and their three children. We had the first floor bedrooms and they had the second floor bedrooms. We shared the bathroom, toilet facilities, kitchen and the wash-house which was in the backyard.

At night, when the sirens went off, it was terrible as my mother and Roselle Le Louarn, the other mother, crammed us all into the cupboard under the stairs or under the table as they were reckoned they were the safest places. Sometimes we were there for three or four hours before the 'all clear' and then it was back to bed only to have it happen again ten minutes later when downstairs we would all go again. I still hate the sound of sirens and if I hear them on television, it gives me the shivers. We could hear the planes overhead and occasionally the bangs of exploding bombs. All the street lights were off and all the windows were blacked out at night.

We lived in that house in Bolton the whole time and we went to school, Devonshire Road Council School, which was a couple of streets away. My mother used to send me to get the bread and I had to queue with the coupons and the lady in the shop used to say to me in her Lancashire accent, "Are you doing the shopping for your mam, luv?" She was a very nice lady.

We made the best of it while we were there, good times or bad, and this other lady who lived with us (Roselle Le Louarn) was a really lovely lady and when she happened to see our Golden Wedding announcement in the Jersey Evening Post three years ago, she sent us a card saying, "I can't believe it, I always remember you as a little child and here you are celebrating your golden wedding." We all lived together for five and a half years: two mothers, two fathers and seven children.

I was 12 when I came back to Jersey. My father came home to help my mother bring us back to Jersey in the September as she could not face the long journey home, but he was not demobbed until about two years after the end of the war. Both our family and the other family each had another baby after the war.

I remember the journey back. We arrived in London, my mother with four children. We had to stay at some rest centre for the night and my mother made quite a fuss because she did not want to share a room with a coloured family, so they put us up in the staff quarters. Then we caught the train that would take us to Weymouth to catch the boat the boat. We travelled on the steamer Hantonia. We were escorted because there were still mines in the English Channel that had not been cleared. It was a terrible, long and rough journey with no comforts whatsoever. I thought it was going on forever.

Once back home in Jersey we went to live in St Martin.

When we had left Jersey we did not know how long we would be away; whether it was weeks, months, years, or even if we would ever come back. It was terrible leaving all our other relations and not knowing what would happen to them in Jersey as there was no contact with them at all throughout the war. Just as we were worrying of them they were worrying about us but we hey were all thinking about us but we all got back together happily, all five years older.

These reminiscences are taken from an interview conducted with Natalie by Jersey War Tunnels.

THE MEMORIES OF GERALD JOURNEAUX

MY name is Gerald Journeaux, and I was born on 12 October 1923, the eldest of three brothers. I went to St Luke's School and then to La Motte Street School.

I left La Motte Street School at 14 years of age and went to work at the Post Office as a telegraph messenger boy, complete with the pillbox hat and the belt, taking telegrams to hotels and so forth. We also delivered telegrams to the Southern Great Western Railway office at 9 Bond Street. In the Channel Islands the offices of the Southern and Great Western Railways who operated the mail steamers were amalgamated. The Southern Railway mailboats, the Isles of Jersey, Guernsey and Sark operated from Southampton and the Great Western vessels, the St Patrick, St David, St Helier and St Julien operated from Weymouth but in Jersey the companies shared the same office. I went to work there for about two months, and then they wanted somebody down on the docks. They had introduced a Scammell mechanical horse which like its animal counterpart was built to tow a trailer and by law, just as with a horse and cart, someone had to ride on the trailer. That was the first type of vehicle they had on the docks and since I wanted an outdoor life, down I went.

On 3 September 1939 war came along but it was not until June 1940 that the British Government (Jersey being a Dependency) decided that the Island should be fortified. Many troops were sent here as well as a couple of aircraft and some anti-aircraft guns. About the second week in June, they decided to declare Jersey an Open Town, so they took everything away. Being an Open Town meant that it was now undefended and it was hoped that would mean that the Germans wouldn't attack because they could have blasted this rock right out of the sea.

I was working on the Southern Great Western Railway then, and they had a curfew on at the time. Working for the Railway, meant we had to move stuff around, sometimes war materials. I've got a piece of paper (probably now the only one in existence) which gave me and other employees of the Railway permission to move around after the curfew. The Entitled Certificate reads that: 'This is to certify that the under-mentioned has permission to proceed from the Airport to New North Quay and his private residence between the hours of 9 pm and 12 midnight'. It carries my name and underneath that 'Vanguard' and 'This Certificate has been issued by the Airports Authority' and it's signed 'For the Flying Officer, Wing Commanding Officer in Charge.' Although not dated, this was issued in the second week of June 1940.

As soon as Jersey was made an Open Town as many of the Islanders as possible gathered down on the Parade, outside the Town Hall, where Bailiff Alexander Coutanche more or less begged everybody not to leave.

As far as my family was concerned, my father, Fred, had fought in the First World War and was still on Supplementary Reserve. When the Second World War broke out those people were called up immediately and so, along with many others, was he. Mothers like mine were left looking after the kids. They never left the Island in those days because no-one had the money to go away. Therefore, with a lot of the fathers in the services and the mothers left with the kids, what would they do? My mother, for instance, was 36 years of age, with three of us, and petrified.

So away we went. We sailed from Jersey on Thursday 20 June 1940 at half past four in the afternoon. I can remember saying to my mother that I was not going and crying my eyes out. I told her that the only way she would get me off this Island was if I could wear my father's best suit. That's true! So she put my father's long trousers on me - I hadn't worn long trousers before. We were on a coal boat named the Porthmorna. There were many other boats that left Jersey at the same time. Most of them went to Weymouth, a tricky journey. We arrived in Weymouth at about seven o'clock the following morning.

When we arrived in Weymouth, we were greeted by some Boy Scouts. They helped us off the boat. We were all weary and carrying everything we had. We had virtually nothing and the Boy Scouts took us to the Central Hall and divided us up.

Some of the families had relations in the United Kingdom, somewhere they could go, but a lot of them went to camps. They were all over England, some of them down in Cornwall, some in Wales. Quite a lot went up to Bolton. Fortunately my mother's sister had married an Englishman who was stationed in England and they lived at Bloxwich near Walsall in the Midlands, so we were able to go up there for a while.

My father was invalided out from the Royal Engineers and since there wasn't enough room for all of us, we went down to Bristol.

When I came of age, I worked for the Bristol Aeroplane Company for a little while working on Beaufort twin-engined torpedo bombers. I did various jobs, like skinning, riveting and assembling things and was on permanent night work. A lot of people there were in tied occupations and they were not called up. We weren't called up either because we were evacuees and exempt. I had got friendly with quite a few lads and some of them did get called up, so I thought to myself, 'I've got to go, got to go', and I volunteered. I was just under 18 I think, and I went to the Recruiting Officer and the fellow there asked me what I wanted to do and where I wanted to go. I told him I'd just come down to volunteer and he could put me wherever he wanted. I said that I was currently at the Bristol Aeroplane Company and not doing anything really special. 'Then you must know something about aeroplanes,' he said, to which I replied 'No'.

'Say no more' he said, 'I'm putting you in the Fleet Air Arm'. So in the Fleet Air Arm I went. I did my bit of service, all over the place.

In 1945, at the end of all the activities, my mother didn't want to go back to Jersey. As all the families in Jersey then were very close-knit and there was all this stupid jabber going on in the Islands (people always talking about other people like they were in a little village) my mother said after her experience in England, she didn't want to return. Being in England had broadened her outlook on life; most of the people that went said afterwards what a secluded place Jersey was. I think the population of Jersey then was not much more than 40,000. I may be wrong on that but there's about 90,000 now

About ten years ago, the Fleet Air Arm Association was formed in Bristol and we were all up there and I was chatting away with a few of the other lads. I told my story and they were telling me theirs and one bloke said to me he was very interested in what I was telling him. So we went a bit deeper, about the ages and the dates and the times. He said, 'I've got news for you, I was one of those Boy Scouts'. He had been there that day down in Weymouth, helping to carry mine or somebody else's gear onto the shore, and I thought that was rather interesting.

The Fleet Air Arm. was originally the Royal Naval Air Service, and it was formed 100 years ago in 1909. Its aeroplanes were on aircraft carriers, although there were some land bases, especially out in the Middle East. I didn't go to the Middle East, but they were all out there and they had the carriers that went with the convoys to Russia and various other places. I was an airframe rigger. We had people who worked on the engines, those who worked on the bodies and those who worked on the armaments. I worked on the bodies.

Our initial training, our foot slogging period, was somewhere near Wigan. About five or six weeks that was, and after that we had to go and take a course up at Hednestford near Cannock Chase in Staffordshire. Then they shipped us off and we went all over the shop. I ended up for quite a while out in the West Indies. Obviously the aircraft parts were made in England, they were crated in England and they were shipped out and we used to assemble them out there in the workshops. Once these aircraft were assembled, to give the pilot taking them on test flights confidence, either the engine mechanic or the airframe mechanic had to go up with him. Obviously if you had to fly in the plane you had just worked on than you would make sure that you did your bit properly. Even little details like split pins could be vital to the plane working properly. What's a split pin? It's a pin put through a hole drilled in a bolt above the nut to make sure the nut doesn't come undone. Today they use spring washers – not so fiddly.

I was demobbed in 1946 and then joined the Police in Bristol, and I have stayed in England ever since.

These reminiscences are taken from an interview conducted with Gerald by Jersey War Tunnels.

BRIAN JOHN LE BRUN
Evacuated from Jersey in 1940, aged 10 years

Following the declaration of war on 3 September 1939, German forces raced across Europe and by the end of May 1940 most of west and eastern Europe was under German occupation. This necessitated the British Government and the States of Jersey in the Channel Islands to give serious consideration to the possible and imminent occupation of the Channel Islands by German forces.

Following consultation it was decided that to try and defend the Islands was not an option and that Islanders were to be given the opportunity to either stay or make use of the evacuation facilities being made available. Time was of the essence. As far as I can remember Islanders were given only 48 hours to decide on their preferred option. I remember everyone being terribly worried about what to do. As my family were in farming thought had to be given, not only to ourselves, but to all the animals. I was one of three brothers aged 6, 10 and 11years, myself being the 10 year old. My father was Stanley Cyril Le Brun and my mother Doris Le Brun (née Blampied). We lived as a family at a rented farm – Alfriston near Haute Croix in the parish of Trinity. Both my mother and father were descended from a long line of Jersey farming families.

Following much discussion and together with my father's brother, his wife and four teenage sons who farmed at Brook Farm, St. John, it was decided that with seven children between them, the two families would evacuate. At the time there were horrendous stories circulating about the Hitler Youth movement and other worries regarding Nazi occupation. The two families just felt that there was no other option but to take up the States' offer and leave the Island. Having made the decision to leave, the nightmare of making the necessary arrangements began. Firstly, I remember my parents having to go to St. Helier to register our intention to leave, before returning to the farm and hastily making arrangements for someone to take care of the farm, including all the animals. As far as I can remember everything was left in the hands of a man employed by my father at the time. Unfortunately this did not work out very well and very soon his relationship with the landlord had deteriorated, resulting in the tenancy being terminated and the farm being sold. My father's brother, who farmed at Brook Farm, fared much better as he owned his farm and another younger brother had offered to look after Brook Farm until the family returned. At that time the thought of us all being away for over five years was not even contemplated.

So to the evacuation itself . Although all this took place 70 years ago and I am now nearing 80 years old, many aspects of the trauma of the time are still very vivid in my mind. I can remember quite clearly us driving down to the Weighbridge, leaving the car there and walking down to the quay. There were several cargo ships tied up ready to take on board all those Islanders who had decided to leave, carrying with them the small amount of baggage permitted. I remember we had to form an orderly queue to board the ships; I remember the metal steps leading down into the ship's hold. We were all sitting or lying on the metal floors as space permitted, before setting sail in the late evening, arriving in Weymouth early the next morning.

On disembarking we were all taken by coach to a local cinema, given tea and sandwiches. There were many officials milling around trying to make our arrival as peaceful as possible. At this point all the evacuees were documented and given the option of either going on a train to Lancashire as part of the official evacuation programme or being independent and travelling separately.

My parents decided to be independent and reservations were made on our behalf at a guest house in Bristol. We had not been there many days before the German Luftwaffe started the huge dock facilities there. Each night the sirens sounded and we were all herded down into the cellars of the large Wills cigarette factory until the all-clear sounded.

Understandably, our stay in Bristol did not last long and we transferred to the Station Hotel in Frome, Somerset – this was a bolt-hole we were to use on other occasions when necessary as we were to move many times during the next five years.

During the following five years on each occasion we moved we took with us everything we possessed, with our parents, my brothers and myself all piled into a canvas-topped Austin Seven. This also meant that my brothers and I were to change schools frequently – not very beneficial to receiving a sound education.

Following a short stay in Frome, my father took up his first job in England on a large mixed farm at Kelmscott, Gloucestershire. This only lasted a few months before he noticed a position on a farm in Avon where there were Jerseys. Unfortunately, this stay was also to be brief as the herd was riddled with Johnes Disease, a fatal wasting disease in cattle, and German bombers made a habit of jettisoning any unused bombs onto the local area following their raids on Bristol Docks. Again this necessitated us all spending many nights under the stairs. We were soon off back to the Station Hotel, Frome, Somerset.

Our next move was to a small village near Ottery St Mary in Devon where we lived in a requisitioned house. My father joined a team working for the Devon War Agricultural Committee, ploughing up thousands of acres of common land and planting potatoes as part of the Government's plans to produce food to feed the United Kingdom population - this was the project called 'Dig for Victory'. The majority of the 'team' lived in caravans on site and I remember one wet Easter, following torrential rain, all those workers whose permanent homes were within a reasonable distance from work went home, knowing that no work would be possible for several days. On their return to the site early on the morning following the Easter holiday the managers were there waiting for them and sacked the whole 'team, including my father, so we were on the move again.

We next went to Shipton-under-Wychwood in Oxfordshire, the home, at the time, of one of the leading herds of Jersey cattle in the UK. The herd actually contained two animals that my father had bred in Jersey. However, the job itself was not with his beloved Jerseys, but as a farm mechanic. As well as being a good farmer and cattle breeder my father was also a dab hand when it came to farm machinery. We were at Shipton for about a year before father took up a position with the Buckinghamshire War Agricultural and Horticultural Committee as Cultivation Officer in Slough. We went to live in a requisitioned house at Burnham in Buckinghamshire, where we stayed for about two years (nearly a record). During this time father rented several small pieces of land where he grew vegetables, supplying produce to local factory canteens and restaurants.

By this time I had reached school leaving age and my first job was to work on the land rented by my father. We grew potatoes (picked by German prisoners of war), cabbages, tomatoes and other vegetables. My elder brother, Denis, had found work on a local farm where we both had Saturday morning jobs, usually carting water around to the local fields stocked with cattle and sheep. We had both thoroughly enjoyed doing this on a Saturday morning, earning the grand total of 2/6d (circa 12p) each.

At the war's end we moved from Buckinghamshire. Thanks to the tenancy on our farm in Jersey having been terminated, my father took on the tenancy of a 160 acre farm at Tilehurst, near Reading, Berkshire, in September 1945. Unfortunately, within three months of taking on this farm, he suffered a massive heart attack and died. However, during the months he was alive he returned to Jersey and purchased eight or ten Jersey cows for shipment to the UK. He was one of the first people to import cattle from the Island following the German occupation. He also managed to get himself appointed as sales representative for Suttons Seeds, one of the leading seed suppliers at the time for the whole of the Channel Islands.

After my father's sudden death, a Mr Wilfred Pipon, also a Jersey evacuee and former Jersey farmer, was appointed farm manager for the farm in Tilehurst. My elder brother and myself were only 16 and 15 years old at the time. Victor, our younger brother, was only 11years old.

This arrangement worked very well for five years until the landlord, a London businessman, decided to sell the farm. Unfortunately, my mother did not have sufficient capital to purchase the property and we had to move – once again. This time a small farm was purchased at Woodley on the other side of Reading.

It became obvious that the farm at Woodley was not big enough to provide a living for us all. I had married by this time and I took up a position on a farm in Jersey which did not prove successful. Following this I was offered a job with a Jersey herd in Devon, but again this proved unsuccessful. Third time lucky, I was offered a position with another Jersey herd in Mapledurham, near Reading. This proved most successful and we remained there for five years. The owner was not only a farmer but also a cattle dealer and was a former Regimental Sergeant Major who had fought all through the war. I learned much during my time in Mapledurham and thoroughly enjoyed his company and the job. Unfortunately, the owner died suddenly and all had to be sold so it was on the move again.

My next position was as a Jersey herd manager on a beautiful estate, Preshaw, near Winchester. I worked here for 11 years for Sir Alwyne Pelly, Bart, a true gentleman. During this time I visited Jersey on many occasions buying cattle and the herd became one of the leading show herds in the UK, winning four Royal Show championships together with championships at most leading shows in the South of England.

However, all good things come to an end and following changes in the management, disillusionment started to set in. I was then offered a position with another Jersey herd near Eastleigh with the possibility of a partnership, which I accepted.

After about four years it was decided that a larger farm was required to accommodate herd numbers which had then risen to about 100 milking cows plus followers. Thus a 240 acre farm in Dorset was purchased by the partnership in 1975. We moved over 200 animals and all farm machinery, which proved quite an undertaking and very challenging. We farmed in Dorset for just over two years before the serious drought of 1976 began to take its toll and with my senior partner nearly 80 years of age and myself starting to have health problems, it was decided, following professional advice, to call it a day. A very successful sale of both the farm and livestock was held in July 1977. Following the sale of the farm in Dorset we moved to Bedfordshire to work with a Jersey herd for a short spell; quite a change from the rolling hills of Dorset.

A position became available with the Jersey Cattle Society of the UK as Field Officer which I undertook in late 1978. As the office was in Reading this necessitated buying a property within easy reach. We settled in Thatcham, about 15 miles from Reading, where we still live.

It was a huge transformation to go from milking cows to an office environment, although Field Officer duties did mean making farm visits and travelling the length and breadth of the country. I soon slipped into this new environment, so much so that by 1986 I was made Assistant Secretary, followed shortly afterwards by being appointed Company Secretary, a post which I held for six years until my retirement in 1994.

During my fifteen years with the Jersey Cattle Society I had the privilege of being invited to judge Jerseys at many agricultural shows, including three in Jersey, twice at Springfield showground and also when the show was held at the Hotel de France. I also had the honour of officiating at the UK Royal Show in 1995 and also in Kenya, New Zealand and South Africa . The Jersey cow has taken me to many countries around the world, including Denmark, Kenya, New Zealand, Australia, South Africa, Costa Rica, Canada and the USA through the World Jersey Cattle Bureau.

I owe a lot to the Jersey cow. Not only did she take me around the world, but from a very shaky start in 1940, I feel the Jersey cow has given me a most enjoyable life, for which I am most grateful.

I feel it is important that I add details of how the rest of my family fared, especially my two brothers, Denis and Victor. My mother, Doris, lived in Oxfordshire for most of her life after my father died. She lived to the ripe old age of 90, never re-marrying.

Denis, my elder brother, died in 2005 aged 77. He also had a very successful career with farming and Jersey cows. Like myself he worked with Jersey herds in the south of England, ultimately being appointed Herd Manager for Mr Michael Richards in Hertfordshire for whom he worked for more than 20 years. He developed the herd entirely on Island bloodlines and this became one of the leading UK Jersey herds. Denis won the Championship at the Royal Show on many occasions, together with many other leading shows in the South of England. He was also appointed to the UK Judges Panel and was also honoured to have officiated at the Island Shows on several occasions.

Victor, my younger brother, started his working life in farming but decided after a few years that farming was not for him. Like our father he was also able to turn his hand to things mechanical. Victor took up a position with a leading motor trader in Oxford. He started by washing and valeting cars for sale and culminated a very successful career as Commercial Sales Manager. He retired after 35 years' service and still resides in Oxford. We keep in close touch.

TIMELINE

Year	Place
1940	Jersey to Weymouth
1940	Weymouth to Bristol
1940	Bristol to Kelmscott, Glos.
1940/41	Frome, Somerset
1941/42	Alfington, near Ottery St Mary, Devon
1942/43	Shipton-under-Wychwood, Oxon
1942/45	Burnham, Bucks
1945/50	Tilehurst, near Reading, Berks
1950/52	Woodley, near Reading, Berks

1952/53	Jersey
1953/54	Chudleigh, Devon
1954/58	Mapledurham, near Reading, Berks
1958/1969	Preshaw, near Southampton, Hants
1969/1975	Fair Oak, Eastleigh, Hants
1975/77	Crewkerne, Dorset
1977/78	Leighton Buzzard, Beds
1978	Started working at Jersey Cattle Society of the UK, Reading
1994	Retired from JCS

1978 to present day Resident in Thatcham, Newbury, Berkshire

Brian Le Brun

MY EVACUATION STORY - EARLY JUNE 1940
by EDWARD G. LE CONTE

I evacuated from the Albert Pier early in June 1940 when I was 20. I left with a life-long friend Denis Griffiths, also 20, a gentleman from London. We sailed on a guano boat to Weymouth. It was a long uneventful journey of 12 hours on a smooth sea.

On arrival we were taken to a cinema where we were given a medical examination by an Army Medical Officer who asked us what we intended to do. We replied "join the armed forces" which was the social obligation expected of young men of military age just after the retreat of Dunkirk.

So we repaired to a Mr and Mrs Clifford Davis of 19 Charlwood Road, Putney, London, as Denis was a friend of their son Jack who was now a Chief Petty Officer in the Royal Navy.

We found a Recruiting Office at Horn Lane in Acton and joined a front line Regiment The Sherwood Foresters which became our Parent Unit. We had to wait a fortnight until a draft of recruits was called up to the headquarters at Normanton Barracks, Derby, for six months' infantry training.

While waiting we visited many places of interest - Lord's, The Oval, 10 Downing Street, Madame Taussards, Selfridges, Oxford Street, Regent Street, Trafalgar Square, Hyde Park, Rotten Row, Edgware and Bayswater Roads, Marble Arch, the Royal Albert Hall, the National Gallery and the Boat Race course towpath from Putney to Mortlake, the Thames Embankment and the precincts of the Houses of Parliament.

The day duly arrived to report to the gate of Normanton Barracks, Derby, which was a four hours rail journey from St Pancras.

The first soldier we met was L/Cpl Webber, a Midlands man who had served in Kingston, Jamaica, and he showed us to our quarters in the relevant Nissen hut which was the future home for the draft of 30 recruits.

After six months' infantry training, we were posted to the 13th Battalion stationed on the east Essex coast at Southend, but Denis and I were split up - Denis to 'B' Company with a Major Adkins and myself to 'C' Company with a Major John Craig. Various military duties followed, barbed wiring and long hours on guard with two hours on and four hours off duty for a spell as long as two weeks.

Denis volunteered for a transfer to the 1st -5th Battalion to make them up to strength to travel abroad. Meanwhile I soldiered on in 'C' Company by then employed as Company Clerk, eventually sailing to India on 2 May 1942 from Clydebank on board the 32,000 ton liner Britannic.

It took eight weeks to sail to Bombay. I served for six months at Rawalpindi in the Punjab and for two years altogether with the Royal Armoured Corps (39th) at Lake Lines, Balarum and at a "Lakindit" training camp with the 1st Bn Essex Regt situated at the Ken River, Central Provinces of India. With every column there was a platoon of Royal Engineers and also a platoon of Gurkhas.

I went into action behind Japanese lines on 2 May 1944 on the Assam/Burma border in the Naga hills in the foothills of the Himalayas. I was involved in two ambushes, a night fighting patrol, a fixed bayonet attack and was bombarded on three occasions by an enemy 6" mortar in conditions that can only be described as 'pure Hell on Earth'.

Cpl Edward le Conte, aged 26
at Poona, India
October 1945, during World War Two

The Campaign of No 56 Column "Chindits" (Essex Regt) of
The "Forgotten" Army, Japanese-occupied Burma, 2 May 1944
until 15 August 1945

It was a miracle that the Burma Campaign came to a successful conclusion because of the insurmountable differences of the four great leaders Archibald, Lord Wavell, Viceroy of India, Field Marshal Sir William Slim, US General Joe Stilwell, who could not stand the sight of the British, and Generalissimo Chiang Kai Shek, the Chinese leader.

However, my contribution commenced on 2 May 1944 when I marched into Japanese-occupied Burma with a party of sixteen personnel under the leadership of a Lieut Swallow and a L/Cpl Sylvester, from the Manipur Road, a distance of eight miles, to join the 56 Column "Chindits" situated north east of Kohima, where a fierce battle was raging. After twenty minutes or so a youth of around eighteen years of age, fair and slim, collapsed and fainted with fright. Upon recovery he was sent back by Lieut Swallow to India with L/Cpl Sylvester,

On arrival at the column I was posted to a section led by Cpl McDowell, who was very ill with malaria and dysentery, and who was carried back to India by three Naga tribesmen on an improvised stretcher made from slender tree branches and ground sheets. He was replaced by a Cpl Kemp, a very brave N.C.O. who was not always scrupulously fair with the rations.

The platoon commander was a Lieut Jack Donaldson (a Scotsman), a very good officer, cool, careful, but firm, who I liked. My 'baptism of fire' was at the Naga village of Nerkima where the Japanese mortared the column on three occasions from Chesurima, an adjacent village. The column commander, Lieut Col Alec Lovelace, a Hastings field officer, sent over a few hundred rounds of .303 Armstrong Vickers machine gunfire in reply.

My next action was at a village named Salapur in a platoon ambush. It was reported that a Japanese section was approaching the village, so we mounted an ambush on the hillside overlooking the muddy track leading to the village, but a Guernsey mortar officer, Lieut Le Cheminant, inadvertently made a footprint on the muddy soil and a private soldier accidentally fired a round of ammunition and although we laid in ambush for an hour, the enemy did not appear, which was just as well!

The next action was in an ambush 400 yards or so to the north of Sinchin, a Naga village situated on a mountain ridge 6,000 feet above sea level, which continued to 7,000 feet.

We were heavily mortared by the enemy and Lieut Donaldson shouted 'Get out of it – every man for himself!'. So we made a hasty withdrawal and as I was running down the track with Pte George Parsons, a postman from Belper, Derbyshire, who incidentally was with me throughout the Second World War, a Japanese mortar shell fell six feet away from us in long grass and did not explode. So we continued to Sinchin, collected our kit and bivouacked a quarter of a mile to the south. After an early breakfast of American K rations, we advanced cautiously at dawn to the village of Sinchin. Lieut Donaldson gave the order to fix bayonets, then he sent in Pte Venables, a regular soldier, to the right of the village to draw the enemy's fire. Then he sent me in and came right behind me with a loaded Tommy gun under his right arm and a Mills hand grenade in his left hand. I shielded him. When he came approximately ten yards away from the open window of the first Naga 'basha', he lobbed the grenade through the open window, then he said to me "go in with the fixed bayonet" which I did and thankfully the

Japanese had withdrawn, so Lieut Donaldson and myself recaptured the village and called the remainder of the platoon in.

We consolidated for two days then proceeded to Onchin, where the column was bivouacked. One of our men, Pte Ernie Nyce, was suffering from malaria, dysentery and typhus with a temperature of 104° and two men, Ptes Stevenson and Jenkins carried him, one each side, and I carried his "big pack" containing rations and ammunition all the way to Onchin, besides my own, descending 6,000 feet across a fast flowing river with rapids and boulders, by a rough bridge of slender tree trunks made by the Royal Engineers platoon.

From there we marched out, via the large village of Ukheul and the Somra Plateau to Imphal on 27 September 1944, after 148 days in action.

Here were actually two Japanese surrenders. A General Kimura disdainfully surrendered to a General Stopford in northern Burma and after the atom bombs were dropped on Hiroshima and Nagasaki, the Japanese High Command surrendered to the American General Douglas MacArthur on USS Missouri in Tokyo Bay on 15 August 1945.

Major General Orde Wingate derived the word "Chindit" from 'Chinthe', the name of the Burmese God that, in the form of a golden lion, guards the entrance to Burmese Temples and this word is now firmly established as part of the English vocabulary. In fact it was all Wingate's brainchild and he was sadly killed in action in a flying accident, early during the campaign.

Altogether I had two comrades killed and five wounded and was in fact a Sherwood Forester (Notts and Derbys). was transferred to the "Chindits" and the Essex Regt where I was promoted to the rank of full corporal. Major General Orde Wingate D.S.O. himself came from Warwickshire.

I am pleased to relate that Pte Ernie Nyce recovered from his three tropical illnesses and Pte Venables was awarded a B.E.M. for his bravery in drawing the enemy's fire.

Edward G Le Conte, Chindit Medal with 1944 Bar
Ex/Chindit N.C.O., Burma Star
Insurance Diploma (London) G.S.C.
Friend and Benefactor of the Gurkhas
Peninsular Barracks (Winchester) Hants

Edward Le Conte aged 26, Poona, India, October 1945

THE MEMORIES OF PATRICIA DONNE DAVIS née MILLER OF AN EVACUATION WITH A DIFFERENCE

I was born in Guernsey on 26 June 1940, two days before the Island was bombed by the Germans. Mothers in the maternity hospital were told to get their babies from the nursery, in case it was hit. My father was working at the harbour and a workmate just feet away from him was killed in the attack. I could have been fatherless at just two days old!

My father, Dick Miller, was a Guernseyman and he met my mother, Marjorie Bird from Bird's Bakery in St Helier, after a Muratti football match in Jersey in the 1930s. They married in 1938 and settled in Guernsey.

By 1942 mother was expecting again. My father didn't want to work for the Germans and food shortages were making life hard. My mother's family must have suggested that they try to get to Jersey, where the bakery business made things a little easier. I remember my parents telling me they had to see the German Commandant to get permission and this was granted, with the condition that they could not return to Guernsey. My mother's brother Harold then applied to the Jersey Commandant and managed to get permission to take a pantechnicon to Guernsey to bring back all their furniture. I still have their solid oak dining table and chairs, together with the bill showing they were hand-made in London in 1938 for the princely sum of £14.10s.0d. They were not given a specific day to travel and had to keep going to the harbour to see if there was a boat going to Jersey.

Eventually, on 23 April 1942, a lovely sunny day, we left Guernsey on a former river barge. I was 22 months old and my mother told me that the German sailors were kind and piled boxes of Guernsey flowers around my pram to shade me from the sun.

It must have been a relief to arrive safely and to show me off to my Jersey grandparents for the very first time.

During the rest of the occupation my father worked at the Summerland factory, making shoes and sabots and after the Liberation he joined the family bakery doing the delivery rounds. My parents were a very happy loving couple and had 61 years of married life together.

I'm not sure how many people were allowed to move from one island to the other during the occupation, or if we were just very lucky to have been given permission to do so. Certainly at every census the apparent inconsistency between my place of birth and number of years residence in Jersey is always queried !

THE MEMORIES OF JUNE LE GROS née BARTON

MY name is June Le Gros and I was born to my parents Herbert William and Edna Barton (née Rondel) on 15 June 1936. Three years later, my sister, Pamela Mary, was born on Good Friday, 7 April 1939.

Since I was only four years and a few days old when we were evacuated, I don't remember much, but I do remember living with my mother and father. I was born at Havre des Pas, and later we moved to Roseville Street. I can remember the house there quite clearly but not a lot more. Obviously it was discussed whether we should leave and my father said that we had to go. He planned to close down where he worked and follow us. In the event, we sailed on the last boat so he was left behind in Jersey for the entire occupation.

My father was a gardener and worked at Belvedere House, which is no more. There was also a connection with the Links Estate, the Stewart family, but I don't know whether it was the Links he had to go and close up, or whether it was Belvedere.

I have always understood that we left on the last boat out around the 21 June 1940 , and the family who left were my mother, sister and myself, my maternal grandmother, her brother, who was a widower, and his son who was a few years older than me. I've got an idea that he actually joined the forces when he was old enough.

The recollection I have is going to a place called Parkstone, between Poole and Bournemouth, because my mother knew a couple who lived there. How we got the house, or where we went or for how long, I just don't recall.

However, we lived in a very nice house, although I haven't been in it since. I have passed it and seen it still standing on the Sandbanks Road.

Sandbanks is now a very smart district. The people that we knew there were obviously friends, but I don't think it was their house we moved into. Presumably we had to pay rent for I know my mother went out to work because otherwise we would have had no income but as my grandmother was there too, she was able to look after my sister and me.

There were six of us and, as far as I remember, we all stayed together, my uncle and cousin living with us. I can still see part of that house; it was a reasonable size, and must have had three bedrooms but I think the bathroom and toilet were downstairs. I don't know how mother found it, or whether she paid rent or if she did, to whom. I do know, however, that she went out to work in a grocer's shop but I can't remember the name of it. I know she was able to bring back bits and pieces like a few extra slices of bacon or occasionally a couple of eggs. We never went hungry.

There was a small garden attached to this house and we grew some vegetables. I know that at one time we also had a few chickens laying eggs. They just scraped around, but I presume she fed them with something. Then we got rabbits. My mother didn't eat poultry or game and once the rabbits were fully grown, she would take them to the butcher who killed them and give her something in exchange. I remember her telling us that. I can't ever remember feeling hungry.

We had no contact at all with my father for the whole time other than a Red Cross letter. I believe my mother managed to get one through either to him or from him, via a cousin who was in the forces, the Parachute Regiment. That was the only contact we had. When I did eventually meet him, he was a stranger. I didn't remember him at all, neither did my sister who was only eighteen months old when we left Jersey.

We started going to a little nursery school. I call it a nursery school, but in fact at first it was just a lady who had a son and a daughter of similar age and we started off in this lady's sitting room. Her name was Mrs Murray and she was a qualified teacher, so she took us under her wing and it grew a bit like Topsy. Eventually she opened a little school and we continued going there throughout the war. Buckholme Towers School is still there and we went past and saw it some time ago. I wrote to them and they sent me some lovely literature, showing how well it was doing. I feel as though I was a founder pupil!

There was an epidemic of mumps while we were there and the school (we were calling it a school by then) had to close down in case the teachers caught it. My mother got the mumps and although my sister and I slept with her hoping to get them, to this day I have never had mumps!

I went to elocution lessons. I was always quite tall, and I can remember I had to walk with a book on my head. I could do it quite well and everybody used to say I was a 'flathead'. I suppose the book was because I was tall and carrying it on my head improved my posture to get the air flow for the delivery of speech. I remember we did a play, Queen of Hearts, and I played the Queen. Somewhere I've got pictures of all of us dressed up.

We used to go swimming down at Sandbanks and there was a man-made lake in Poole Park which we would cross in a little boat. There was a railway track at the side of the house and trains passed by just a stone's throw away.

I remember air raids quite distinctly, because it was always me who seemed to wake up when the siren went off. We had to evacuate the house and were not allowed to shine any lights because of the blackout, so when we went down the garden path to the Anderson shelter, although it wasn't very far, we would be hanging on to each other as we went.

But after a while the shelter got so wet and unpleasant that my Mother got a metal Morrison shelter which we installed in a room and used as a table in the corner. There was a mattress underneath it and that's where my sister and I used to sleep.

Mother joined an organisation for women, a bit like the Home Guard. One night she went out and a German plane crashed quite near where we were. She spoke afterwards about seeing the pilot emerging from it, on fire.

It seems she went through quite a horrific time, one way and another, but she rarely spoke about it, and looking back, if her memories were of people on fire, you can understand why.

We had people who were in the Forces coming to stay with us from time to time because they were pre-war friends of my mother and father. I remember them coming wearing uniforms. Although they weren't relatives, we called them 'Uncle'- I didn't think there was anything sinister in it at the time: you know what I mean!

I can remember one of the 'uncles', Henry Perkins, who was friendly with my mother and father for years after the war, and they even went on holiday together, the three of them, because he never married.

There was a funny little incident that we used to laugh about afterwards. My grandmother had a small case, like a little attaché case, and that always used to go with her to the air raid shelter. Her case contained bank books and silver spoons and silly things like that, but she clung to it as though her life depended on it - she just wanted to know she had it with her. Poor soul, within about 18 months of our coming back, she passed away. She had a stroke and died in her sleep, as quickly as that. But she must have worked hard since she was quite elderly to be looking after two small children under difficult circumstances. I presume she prepared our meals, because my mother was gone quite a lot of the time.

After a while my mother gave up shop work, I don't know why, and she became an agent for the Prudential Assurance Company, knocking on doors collecting premiums. I think she used to ride a bicycle to do that, because she never drove. She didn't drive until well after coming back to Jersey, so I know she didn't have a car, unless she went with somebody who drove. That's what she was doing at the end.

When other evacuees were talking about the Channel Island meetings, I felt as though we too had been to meetings of that kind. Whether these were in Parkstone, Poole or wherever, I wouldn't know. However at one of these meetings I remember singing a hymn For those in Peril on the Sea. I don't know why but that always brought a lump to my throat, perhaps because it reminded me of all that sea between me and my father. Whenever I sing that hymn now, it still chokes me a bit.

We played with the children who lived nearby because we were all of a similar age. I can recall playing on the embankment, it was quite steep, I can't imagine how high, but we were nowhere near the trains even though we were on the actual bank. If we ventured from our own area, it was quite muddy and slushy and I remember my sister falling into horrible mud. At one time I stood on a piece of corrugated iron and it slashed right across my knee. My mother just put a plaster on it and it was repaired. On another occasion I had a nasty fall and I remember splitting my lip. For a few days there was a hard scab there and I couldn't chew my food and I couldn't speak or anything.

At Christmas we always had an orange and an apple and a piece of coal in our stockings. Once we had a dolls' house and a little two wheeled bicycle that stood up on a frame. You turned the pedals and the wheels went round and round and my sister poked her finger in the spokes and nearly lost the top of it. We were in the bedroom, and didn't I get told off! But it was she who put her finger there, not me! Where these presents came from, I have no idea.

We went to Sunday School and also to the Brownies. It was quite strange because the lady that my uncle married had, with my mother, started that Brownie Pack. I am sure they had no idea what they were doing, but at least we went to Brownies during the war. Whether we had uniforms or not, I don't recall, but we probably did.

We went on double-decker buses into Bournemouth to see pantomimes. I was going to a pantomime one evening and I didn't feel at all well. I had awful pains in the top of my legs - I can remember them quite distinctly – but my mother just said it was growing pains. She was very hard in those sort of things, probably because she couldn't afford to have a doctor, so we had to live through the problems. As I got older, I was told there were no such things as growing pains, and each time I had a medical I was asked if I had ever had rheumatic fever. I don't recall having it as such, but those pains in my legs may have been connected. We just lived through it.

We had chicken pox along with some of the children from our nursery school and I got it under my feet. I don't know if you've ever had chicken pox, but it itches and itches, so we used to run about on the gravel to try and get relief under the feet. I am still very sensitive under my feet but I don't know whether it is because of that or not.

We also had measles but, as I have said, never caught the mumps.

I don't remember seeing a dentist and as for seeing a doctor, it was never, ever, ever. We were very lucky, I suppose, because we were all pretty healthy.

At the end of the war, my father came over to England and stayed with us. My parents obviously discussed going back to Jersey. It was no surprise, in a funny sort of way, that we called my father 'Uncle' when we first encountered him! He stayed for some time but whether he had to find his own way, was given compassionate leave from his job as a gardener or came without wages, I've no idea. Those were questions I didn't ask.

When we returned to Jersey we moved into a little cottage adjacent to Belvedere House. In fact you could barely call it a cottage. It was only a two up, two down, with an outside toilet. It had been built, or converted, into what was going to be the laundry for Belvedere House, so there was a boxed in bath in what was both our kitchen and sitting room. My mother did everything in that one room although there was another little anteroom that held a piano and not much else. We had two decent sized bedrooms upstairs. And that was it.

That's where we lived until I got married in 1960.

My uncle had married by the end of the war and stayed in England and my cousin also stayed. I don't think he was married then but he did get married later and he and his wife only returned to Jersey for holidays.

I should have sat the 11-plus in England with all my contemporaries but I came back and within a couple of months had to take it in Jersey where, at that time, it included French. I had never learnt a word of proper French, but before we evacuated and even though I was only four years old, they used to say I could speak more Jersey-French than English. If my mother and grandmother didn't want us to understand what they were talking about, they spoke in French. Often, when we were on buses or out and about and they wanted to talk about someone, they would gossip about them in French.

When we came back to Jersey my mother could still speak Jersey French although with a name like Barton everybody wanted to know how she knew it.

Back in school in Jersey, every child in our class wrote us a letter but I didn't keep in touch with any of them, which was a shame. Interests change and it's got to be a two-way thing. It's no good one person writing constantly and not the other.

I used to write a lot to various people; I had a pen friend, and kept in touch with one of the girls we were friendly with who lived a couple of doors away in Parkstone. I kept in contact with her. She married, and had a daughter, but unfortunately has since died. She lost her husband and now she's gone as well. Her daughter still maintains contact. She's married; her husband is Japanese and she has had a baby in Japan. I still keep in touch with her, so there is still a link with my war-time experiences.

Mrs Murray who started the school has gone, because I was sent a cutting to say that she had died.

My mother and father have both died and my sister has passed away as have my various cousins, so it's just me now.

That's about it, I think. It's surprising that when you start thinking about it how much comes flooding back. It just needs somebody to ask the questions.

These reminiscences are taken from an interview conducted with June by Jersey War Tunnels.

June and Pamela

THE EXPERIENCES OF ENA AVRIL PERRIER née Crosby

These are my experiences as one of the evacuees leaving on the last boat in June 1940 . I think the boat was called Arcangel.

In April 1940 I had had my eighth birthday when I was given my first bicycle and a white kitten I called Snowy. My father had been in France in 1939-1940 and was lucky to have been rescued at Dunkirk. He came home for a short leave and left not knowing that we would follow shortly after. My first day as an evacuee started with a family friend coming to take my kitten and our dog for a ride in his van and, of course, they never came back. I later learnt they had gone to be put down.

My mother had to put a few things together in a small case and I was told to get dressed, which I did by putting on my FCJ school uniform thinking I was going to school. Then our family friend came back to collect us in his van to take us to town. My grandmother and aunt (my father's sister) who stayed in Jersey with her newborn baby girl were crying and I could not understand why.

My mother's sister and her two sons, my cousins aged eight and ten, were waiting for us. I forgot to mention my mother and aunt came from Yorkshire which is why we had to leave the Island, we later learnt had we not left the Island then we would have been sent to a prisoner of war camp. I remember holding my cousin George's hand while his brother Charlie held their mother's hand (Dingle was their surname).

It was a nightmare boarding. The ship was a coal boat, as they were using everything that would float to get the last people away. We were very fortunate as our boat was heading straight to England.

There was no room on deck so we had to go down a ladder into the hold where we had to stay put. It was quite dark down there and the only toilets were a row of tin buckets and I still remember the awful smell.

We seemed to be on that boat forever. There was no food as we had rushed to leave, until someone came around with a box of ship's biscuits that were so hard that we soaked them in the cold water that we had been given to drink.

When we arrived we were eventually herded into a large building where a nice lady appeared with a large trolley and gave us sandwiches, cakes and tea which we gratefully gobbled up as we were so hungry!

We had a quick medical and a label with my name and destination was pinned onto my school blazer.

From then on we went to the station to catch a train for Leeds. It was another long journey but we had a few stops at stations where my mum and aunt were able to buy some food and drink at the station buffet. We also had some stops on route for air raids but thankfully we did not get hit.

We reached Leeds where we were met by another aunt and uncle then took a bus journey to their house in Menston. The following day we all caught the bus to Bradford where we went to live at 612 Thornton Road with my grandparents. We stayed there for about eight or nine months.

My mum and aunt had to go to work at a munitions factory and we three children were found a school, not a very pleasant experience for me. On my first day the teacher stood me up in front of the class and said "we have a new girl; she is a refugee from Jersey". No-one knew where that was. From then on, while at that school, I was called "Refugee" and not by my name.

During this time our grandmother was very ill with cancer and we children had to go and kiss her goodnight every night. Mum told us to hold our breath because the smell was stomach curdling. This was still in 1940 as my grandmother died in October that year. My grandfather lived only a short time longer.

This meant we were on the move again. The two boys were split up and went to two different aunts and uncles of the family for the duration of the war.

When we moved to Guiseley near Leeds, Mum and I went to Scotland for a couple of months as my father was stationed there, waiting to be sent overseas. So it was another school for me (the second in less than a year) and another temporary home for us.

My father and I used to have nice long walks in the countryside and I did enjoy that short time I had with him. I can remember walking in a field when we saw two men with nets and ferrets. They were catching rabbits. My dad went to help them and I can still hear the screams from those poor rabbits. I remember crying all the way home where we were staying and my mother was furious with my father for letting me see that. After that my father was sent overseas and we did not know where, so we returned to Guiseley

We had to stay with relatives for a while until the Council found us somewhere to live. It was yet another school for me and another munitions factory for my mother. I could only stay at the school until I was 11, so it was only a matter of time before I had to move again, making it four schools in five years (not bad eh?)

The Council soon found us somewhere to live in a long row of cottages in Union Street. I learned later that the whole street was due for demolition for rebuilding before the war. Then the war started so it was put on hold.

Mum told me years later she really cried when she saw the state of it, with holes in the wall stuffed with paper and old rags to keep the draught out, bare floors, no lino and paper peeling off the walls (which we pulled off). In the scullery was an old stone sink with a bucket underneath, only a cold water tap, a rusty cooker (with Queen Anne legs), which I was told never to touch since it was a gas cooker. There was a wire-fronted box on the wall and I believe this was used as a meat safe. We had no furniture but were given a bed with linen, a single wardrobe and a chair for the bedroom. Downstairs we were given a small table, one chair and a stool for me and a fireside chair for my mother. My aunt gave us a rag rug; these were still being made by the older ladies. There was a small fireplace. When you put on four pieces of coal, it overflowed but at least it gave us some heat! It was lovely in the winter when I had a bath in the old tin bath my mother had found in the shed adjoining the toilet at the bottom of the garden.

This was home for us until the war ended. Thank goodness my father never saw it. I think he would have gone straight to Germany to throttle Hitler!

Life went on and my mother went to work while I went to school. Of course, children were relatively safe and free, in an old sense, and we could play outside. We played hopscotch, catch-me-if-you-can, skipping (my skipping rope was a surplus end of a clothes line – but it worked), a whipping top and lots of ball games. I had three tennis balls given to me, they were very bald, but they bounced on the wall and on the floor! We girls would sometimes sit on the doorstep and chat.

Clothes were a problem. I was very hard on shoes so my mother bought me some clogs. You did not have to use coupons for those like you did for all our other clothes. My clogs were nice, they were green and had brass studs, they made a lovely sound when you walked and if you kicked really hard on the cobbles you sometimes got a spark. I am surprised mine never caught fire!

On a Saturday morning if you had two pennies to spend all the children used to go to the local shop and buy a small bag of broken biscuits. The shopkeeper made these up for us and it did not come off my mother's ration book. It was great if you found a small piece of broken chocolate in your bag, but it did not happen very often.

On a Saturday afternoon we would go to the picture house. Rain or shine, you had to go. I loved the films and cartoons. Sometimes the air raid sirens sounded and everyone went to the shelters, but I don't remember having any bombing during the later stages of the war.

It must have been very traumatic for a parent or parents to cope with a family during these times and as for children like myself, it was very frightening because you had suddenly left your home and friends and everything you were familiar with to find yourself living in a strange place with strangers and having to cope as best you could.

I didn't have any toys so I made a dolls house from a cardboard box, cutting out the door and windows and the furniture I made from matchboxes. I was a good reader so I had lots of books and Enid Blyton being my favourite.

This was my life until 1945 when we came home.

I still think we were very lucky to be on one of the last boats to leave and also to be in Yorkshire, even though I was a latchkey child (door key on a ribbon around my neck).

You had to grow up fast in these conditions. I made a lot of friends but lost contact after we came back to Jersey. I have one special friend who name is Marguerite whom I met during the war when I was 10 and she was nine years old. We have remained friends for more than 60 years.

I know there are a lot of evacuees still alive in the Island who have their own stories to tell; some good, some bad, but this is my story as I remember it. I was eight years old when we left Jersey and 13 when we returned, and, of course, I had to go back to school for two more years.

Some people referred to us as "rats leaving a sinking ship" but everyone was frightened not knowing what life was going to be like under a German occupation. I am just glad I am still here to be able to write this.

THE MEMORIES OF BETTY STATT née Crapp

In June 1940 my father, Ted Crapp, left the Island with the intention of joining the Army. Once the Army found out he had four children, he was told to get work in the aircraft industry. He immediately sent a telegram to my mother telling her "to come at once".

On Friday 28 June 1940, my mother, Lily (née Horn), sister Muriel aged 14, brothers Denis 13, and Leslie just five, and me, Betty, almost 10, left the Island on the last mailboat, the ss Isle of Sark, all our fares being paid by my maternal grandfather.

We sailed to Guernsey where it was decided it would be safer to cross the English Channel at night because of the threat of U-boats.

We went ashore at St. Peter Port going to a café for lunch. This was the first time that my siblings and I had left Jersey and also visited a café! After our lunch we walked around for a while until Leslie started crying and refused to walk up any more hills, which was very understandable as it was a very hot day and we were all wearing as many clothes as possible.

My mother decided we would return to the boat, but once there we had to dash inside it as a plane started machine gunning the harbour and we could hear bombs dropping. When the raid was over we saw all the tomato lorries on the pier ablaze. This was very frightening and our first introduction to air raids.

After travelling overnight we arrived at Southampton and caught a train to Bristol, followed by a seven mile bus ride to Patchway, with a long walk to my aunt's cottage and a reunion with my father. All six of us had to share a double bed, three at the top and three at the bottom, until we managed to rent a house near the aerodrome and, with the help of neighbours, H.P. payments and the Salvation Army, we were able to obtain the bare necessities of life.

On the Monday my mother went to the Post Office to send a telegram home to Jersey to say we had arrived safely, only to be told that the Germans were already there. She had to be given a chair and a glass of water as she almost fainted with shock.

My father worked for the Bristol Aeroplane Company (B.A.C.) which had factories in Patchway and Filton. Later he became a Special Constable (an honorary policeman but with a uniform).

My mother became a member of the Women's Voluntary Service (WVS) and also worked as a filing clerk in the factory. Muriel, who had been at the Intermediate School and missed all her friends, became a cashier in a big store in Bristol which she enjoyed, but unfortunately it was destroyed in the blitz. She then did office work at B.A.C. and 'fire-watching' as a member of the St John Ambulance Brigade, but before her uniform arrived she joined the Auxiliary Territorial Service (A.T.S.) later being promoted to sergeant. She also met a Bristolian serviceman from the Royal Army Service Corps (R.A.S.C.) who later became her husband.

Denis had to go to school until he was fourteen and then he too went to work at the Bristol Aeroplane Company. He joined the Home Guard and later joined the Merchant Navy during which time he served in both the Atlantic and Pacific Oceans, sailing round the world twice.

Leslie and I went to Patchway Council School. I was lucky enough to find a friend straight away as she had just moved to get away from the bombing in Bristol, and that helped me as I missed the beaches and Havre des Pas bathing pool. Later I went to Thornbury Grammar School which was a seven mile bus ride away. Just before we left Bristol to come home, Leslie passed his 11 Plus exams.

We endured many air raids and for one spell we all slept downstairs in the kitchen, partly under the kitchen sink, as it was too dangerous to be upstairs.; some nights we spent in our neighbours' air raid shelter. Later we had an indoor Morrison shelter installed in our kitchen, - we actually used it as a table top since the air raids had finished by then.

Despite all the trials and worries, morale was kept up by the BBC who transferred their broadcasting services from London to Bristol, which gave us the opportunity to see occasional shows at the Colston Hall. On one occasion the popular singer Bruce Trent (who was born in Jersey) sang "Beautiful Jersey" at the Bristol Hippodrome.

We often put up Jersey servicemen during their leave most of whom were former members of Springfield Sports Club, as many of them had no family in England and very few people to visit.

Finally on Saturday 30 September 1945, my parents, Leslie and I flew back to the Island in a small plane from Southampton and were reunited at the airport with the family we had not seen for more than five long years.

THE EXPERIENCES OF REG STATT
as told by his widow Betty

My late husband, Reg Statt, left the Island with his mother and they travelled to England on a coal boat. On arrival in England, as they did not have anywhere to go, they were sent to Bolton with a group of other evacuees.

It was about three weeks before Reg's 14th birthday and his dream of becoming a motor mechanic was shattered. He had to go out to work and eventually went into the cotton mills until he was conscripted into the Army. He was in India when the war ended and returned to England, but he was demobbed early and had to return to the cotton mills to finish his time there.

Two things then happened which changed his life for ever. One of the girls at the mill with a "Veronica Lake" hairstyle, caught her hair in the machinery and was left with only half a head of hair and blood pouring down her face, something he never forgot. Two weeks later he witnessed a motor cycle accident and both occasions left him with a feeling of utter helplessness as he did not know what to do or how he could have helped..

So he joined the Bolton St John's Ambulance Brigade, and when he returned to the Island he joined the local St John's Ambulance Brigade at the very first opportunity. He stayed with the service for 36 years until his retirement.

THE MEMORIES OF IRIS TIERNEY née Diment

An expectant hush fell over the crowds in St Helier's Royal Square as the Lt Governor of Jersey, began to speak. Hundreds of people from all parts of the Island had hurried to the square to the public meeting summoned for a hot summer's evening in June 1940. I had never seen the Square so packed nor Jersey people so quiet as they waited for that fateful announcement. When it came it exploded like a bombshell in to the still air.

The Germans were about to invade Jersey and the Island was to be evacuated.

Many stories have been written of wartime heroes and heroines, but I don't think anyone has ever written of the panic and heartbreak caused by the German occupation of the Channel Islands – the only British soil that the Germans held during the war and which prime minister Winston Churchill described on VE-Day as "our dear Channel Islands".

I was only a girl at the time, but I shall always remember that announcement and the almost incredible happenings of the next 24 hours. The evacuation was not compulsory but everyone was advised for their own safety to leave the Island, a thing which many of them had never done in their lives before. That day became D-Day for many families – the Day of Decision. Should they stay on in spite of the threatened German invasion, or leave their homes and belongings and take one of the special boats which were to take them to the mainland? This was the question which had to be answered in the nightmare of the next few hours.

I remember I was working in a large walk-around store at the time, and during the afternoon of Wednesday 19 June 1940, customers came in and told us that a public meeting had been called for that evening and that Jersey had been declared an 'open town'.

None of us had ever dreamed that the Germans would get so near. Though we could hear the gunfire on the coast of France, and often the crockery would fall off the shelves at home with the vibrations, we did not think that we, a part of Britain, could possibly fall into enemy hands.

The afternoon dragged on and at 6.00 p.m. I rushed home to tell my mother the news. My father had already left the Island as he had re-joined the Royal Navy at the outbreak of the war and was serving his country as a gunnery instructor in the training ships on the Thames Embankment. I also had a brother on active service "somewhere abroad".

As I was one of nine children, five of us were still single, Mother decided to try to get the rest of the family who were married and not at home to come into town where we lived for a family conference. This in itself was a difficult task as at the time there was chaos everywhere and they all lived in different parishes in the country. Fortunately, a good friend and neighbour took us by car to their homes to bring them.

After a lot of careful consideration, it was decided at last that we should leave the Island if we had the chance.

I remember my mother's fear of the horror stories she had heard of what would happen to her daughters if we were on occupied territory, and the feeling that her duty to her husband was to take us all to the mainland where at least we should all be together.

The Lt Governor told us that Islanders who wished to leave should queue at the Town Hall for the permits to board the ships which would start to arrive in the harbour the following day. My eldest sister went to get the permit for the whole family and after queuing from 8.00 pm to 11.00 pm, there were only five in front of her when it was declared that no more would be issued until 8 o'clock the following morning! She got down there at 5.15 am and the queue was already a mile long. She finally got our permits as 12 noon.

In the meantime I went home to help sort out the problem of what to do with all our personal belongings. We had been warned that we would not be allowed luggage as space on the ships was urgently needed for passengers. Consequently, we were only allowed a small bundle each.

As we had small children in our family, we decided to leave behind our things in favour of clothing for the babies. This was a bitter disappointment for me personally for just a fortnight before I had been to London for my annual holiday and had bought clothes which I had not yet worn.

We lit a bonfire in the garden that night and burnt personal belongings, papers etc., which we did not want prying eyes to see.

By the time we had finished, we were exhausted and my mother insisted that we should lie down on our beds for an hour or two – though she herself refused to do so. I remember dozing off and jumping up with a start, imagining that I could hear German planes zooming overhead and Germans swarming over my bedroom windowsill.

Very early the next morning I knew I had a dreaded task to do. I had to take our beloved pet, Mickey the dog, to be put to sleep. I was totally unprepared for the sight which met my eyes when I approached the Animal Shelter. There was already a long queue of people with exactly the same thought to spare their pets unnecessary suffering. It was a sight that has stayed with me during the years – those heartbroken owners and their pets. The queue was so long that I could not wait and a kind friend looked after our dog until a later date when they had him put to sleep.

I decided to return home by way of the harbour and find out what ships had arrived. There was no definite time of departure, we just had to be on the pier as soon as we could and take our chance with the crowd.

I remember leaning over the rail and watching in amazement the well-to-do woman bargaining with a Norwegian skipper to take her at once to the mainland with all her belongings. Apparently he was due to sail on the morning tide before the ships came to take the evacuees off, but he was a man of honour and didn't care for her money. He turned to me as I leaned over the rail watching this, and said in broken English. "You are one of big family?" and I replied that I was, he said, "All come down to pier by ten o'clock and I will take you to Newcastle." Unfortunately we were unable to get down to the pier on time so we had to wait our turn.

The day turned out to be one of the hottest of the year and already by noon the heat was unbearable, making all the rushing around, and the hustle and bustle, even more trying. I eventually arrived home to find everyone ready to leave for the pier and evacuation.

As I look back now and think of the moment when we left what was our home and all our possessions to the tender mercy of whoever came after, I must pay tribute to the great courage of my mother. She was just walking out and leaving everything she held so dear – her home – which to most people is everything. It was a waste of time locking doors and windows. We had no idea if we should be gone for one month, one year, or forever.

We arrived at the harbour to find it swarming with people and from the fleet of small vessels it didn't seem possible that half the seething crowd would embark that day. It was a sight made all the more fantastic by people dumping cars, bicycles, prams and so on, over the side of the pier as they realized they had no chance at all of keeping them.

In our family, there were eighteen of us including a six week old baby, and one of twelve months. When we did get to the ship's gangway, one of my elder married sisters and her family decided not to leave the Island. We were heartbroken, and to soothe us she said they would wait a couple of days and see how things turned out, and would come later on. However, they left it too late and so spent the occupation on the Island.

By 5.00 p.m. we had embarked on a small cargo ship. People crammed the decks and you simply could not move. As we sailed out of the harbour into the English Channel, we heard planes overhead and would have panicked had the skipper not explained to us that we had an R.A.F. escort until we got to the English coast.

We berthed in Weymouth at about 1.00 pm the following day and the first thing we had to do was to queue up for a medical examination. The heat was still unbearable and no food was available.

Now we thought of my father who was in London. He would not know whether we had left the Island as communications were impossible on the day we left. We asked numerous times where we were bound for but the officials had obviously been told not to give any information.

There were many curious onlookers watching as the strange cargoes left the ships at Weymouth. Someone asked us who we were and as he was prepared to help, we asked if he could send a telegram to my father. It said simply "Arrived in Weymouth, destination unknown".

After the authorities had got some sort of order, we were taken to a school and given a meal, and then we were taken in buses to the station, still not knowing to where we were going.

I shall never forget the work of the Salvation Army, who filled milk bottles for the babies and passed us food as we pulled in at certain stations. At last, at midnight, we arrived at our destination – a town in Lancashire.

From the train we were taken to yet another school where we were once more supplied with a meal and somewhere to sleep for the night. To us, the people who looked after us were 'Ministering Angels'.

That night will be remembered by many. Very few people in Jersey had ever heard an air raid siren and it seemed that we had hardly got into the building, when this dreadful wailing noise struck terror into everyone's hearts. One mother was so terrified that when she went to pick up her small baby, she dropped it and it died from its injuries. We were ushered out of the school building, across a main road, and to an underground shelter where we remained for what seemed hours. We were told it was a false alarm, which was a great relief to us all after the horror of the past 24 hours.

My mind still returns to the time when so many people left their homes and in some cases part or all of their families.

For what ?

These memories were written by Iris in 1958.

The Houguez Family

JACK AND ADA WILMOTT, ESCAPEES FROM THE CHANNEL ISLANDS

It was May 1940 and barrage balloons were up all round the docks at Southampton when we boarded a ship for Jersey. We had been going there every year for three years to help a farmer friend get in his potato and tomato crops.

It was very dark when we got under way at midnight. We were told to try on our lifejackets, although they had nothing for our five year old son, who was travelling with us. They said if the worst came to the worst, they would do the best they could.

Part way over the Channel everything went quiet. The engines were stopped. They told us not to make a sound as enemy planes were passing overhead en route for the mainland. After a while the engines were started up again and we reached Jersey at 8.00 am, glad to get off the sea.

Our farmer friend was there to meet us, and off we went to work. As the days went by, things on the Island began to get tense. Working up on the côtils, strips of land on the hillsides, we could hear the rumblings of guns and we feared the Germans were getting closer. Then one evening, we heard a great explosion in the sea below us. Someone was trying to bomb the mailboat which had swiftly tacked to avoid it. After that they varied the time the mailboat went out.

In town, things were becoming very unsettled. The potatoes could not be got out, so no money was coming in. The banks had been cleared, and other valuable items removed from the Island, as they knew the invasion was coming.

One Wednesday night news came that Jersey was to be declared an "open island", and British mainlanders or anyone wishing to leave the Island should go and register at the Town Hall in St Helier.

This was four miles from where we were and at seven in the evening we got our young son up and were given a lift into town. When we arrived there they had just declared a curfew, requiring everyone to be indoors or to leave the town.

We walked to some friends and spent the night with them, sleeping on chairs. But we were back on the road at four in the morning when a milk float gave us a lift. At the Town Hall there was a long queue, which we joined. Then we overheard some sailors saying there were people getting away on small boats.

We went to the harbour and were lucky to get aboard one of these. They were calling out for women and children. Jack had our small son in his arms and was told to take him down to me and then come straight up again, which he didn't. He went below to the galley.

It was an old coal boat, very dirty, but we didn't mind that as we were getting away. Crossing the sea was quite frightening, with all sorts of things drifting past. I sat with our son behind a post while Jack brought us up tea from time to time to keep us warm.

We arrived at Weymouth in the early hours of the morning but had to wait until daybreak for them to remove the barriers and let us in.

We were treated well, given food and drink, physically examined and then each given a ticket as refugees. As we had no money, our fares were paid for us to get back to our home in Wisbech.

It was late on a Friday when we reached home. Our families were so pleased to see that we had got away safely. No news had been coming through from us, so they had not known what was going on.

One week later the Germans occupied the Channel Islands, so we were very lucky. We thank God for that.

Forty years later we returned to Jersey to find the children of our friends. This we did and had a lot to talk about. Their eldest son is now a Deputy for the Parish of St John. He took us all around the island and told us about the German Occupation.

Jack went into the Army for five and a half years and sadly died in 2002 leaving me, Ada, with my memories.

THE MEMORIES OF ELIZABETH ETIENNE née FRY

In 1934 my parents Ethel (née Richomme) and Leonard Fry must have thought they were living in heaven. Newly married, by June of that year they were buying their one and only home in the Island at 30 Bellozanne Avenue. I was born on 29 September 1934, while my brother Arthur followed on 18 October 1935. My father was also starting his own business as an auto electrician in Simon Place while my mother looked after the two children.

All this changed on 20 June 1940 and I remember I was staying with Auntie and Uncle Lucas at Modderfield Farm, Maufant, when Mum and Dad arrived and told us to say "goodbye" to them as we were going away on a big boat the next day. I really could not understand why Mum was crying and saying "I will never see Auntie and Uncle again", to which my Dad replied "Of course, you will".

We returned home to Bellozanne Avenue where Mum tried to pack what she could into one suitcase, and the next morning we all went down to the North Quay wearing most of our clothes even though it was a hot day. Arthur and I sat on the suitcase wearily looking at lots and lots of legs in front of us, until eventually our name was called and we all went aboard a very dirty coal boat.

It was very crowded but a sailor pulled out the drawer from underneath his bunk, and Arthur and I lay down in it on top of his clothes. Mum and Dad sat on his bunk and at last Arthur and I fell asleep. Next morning we went on deck and saw the coast of England and eventually landed at Weymouth.

All I remember of Weymouth is sitting on a case loaded onto a trolley and Mum looking after us while Dad went to find someone to talk to about us getting somewhere to stay; I believe it was the Salvation Army who came to our assistance.

While we were waiting a journalist look a photo of us on the case and a few days later it appeared in one of the national newspapers with the caption 'Two little refugees from Channel Islands'. It was only when some of Dad's relations who had already left the Island saw it, that they realized we had arrived in England.

We were sent to an address in Paignton where an old lady ran a boarding house and she was able to give us a room. We stayed there about a month while my father looked for work, and eventually he was sent to the Bristol Aircraft Company factory in Bristol.

Unfortunately, while we were in Paignton, the nail-beds on Arthur's hands turned septic from the dirt from the coal boat, and he had to wear gloves all the time until they were cured.

We were given part of a house in Bedminster but, while there, there were terrible air-raids and once when we were in a brick shelter, a house two doors away from us was bombed and because of the damage to our own house, we had to leave in a hurry.

This time we moved to Patchways where we were lucky to have two rooms and the use of a kitchen and an underground air-raid shelter, in a two bed-roomed house. It was here that I began my schooling and was presented with a gasmask which had to be taken to school every day and I was supposed to take it with me everywhere. I remember how terrible it smelt when I had to wear it, and it used to make me feel quite sick. Most of this time I had to go to school on my own, as Arthur caught diphtheria and had to go to an isolation hospital for six weeks, during which time I was not allowed to go and see him and neither, I believe, were Mum and Dad.

While Arthur was away, Dad built a bunk bed, which was quite wide, in the corner of one of our rooms; Arthur and I were to sleep on the top, whilst Mum and Dad used the bottom layer. As there were nightly air-raids Mum had taken cushions and blankets down to the shelter and tried to make it cosy as invariably about midnight they had to carry us out there and stay until nearly daylight. Miraculously, Arthur used to sleep through all the noise, but I was always awake and used to watch some of our neighbours join us and offer round cups of tea.

I do not think it was a very good thing for Arthur to sleep through all this, as years later when we were back home, he used to have terrible nightmares, thrashing around in his bed and one night nearly knocking out my father who was trying to pacify him. The doctors told my parents it was his subconscious mind reliving the air-raids.

Both Arthur and I were very worried as Christmas approached, because we did not think Father Christmas would know where we were living, and what would he do if he came to the house and we were not in our beds but safe in the shelter. Of course, we need not have worried because he did come and brought us each a stocking with a lump of coal, a sixpenny bit, a sweet and for me a rag doll and for Arthur a small wooden car. What a happy time we had looking into our stockings while still in the shelter.

At the beginning of 1941, once again a house very near to us was bombed and several other houses badly damaged, so we had to leave our home. This time Dad was transferred to the Silver Cross pram factory (which had been converted for the manufacture of aircraft parts) at Guiseley, near Leeds, and we all went to live in a very large house in the village which had several English evacuees living there as well. I am told that my mother organized them by helping them with their cooking, and general housework, and this was greatly appreciated by them all. Although Dad never told me this, he did tell one of his brothers-in-law, and said how proud he was of Mum. What a pity he never told Arthur and me!

While living in Guiseley, Arthur and I both went to the hospital to have our tonsils out, and I think this was the first time I remembered having jelly for tea. During the winter we both had very bad colds, and as there were some workmen tarring the road nearby, Mum went and asked for two lumps of tar, which she wrapped up in red flannel and which we wore around our necks for several weeks.

Later that year, Dad was again moved to another factory near Eccleshill, just three miles from Bradford, and here we stayed at 72 Stonehall Road for the remainder of the war.

Arthur and I used to walk to Undercliff School, and on the way we had to carry a large glass battery from Dad's radio set for the garage to refill ready for us to collect on the way back. Arthur had a metal hoop with a short stick which he used to roll all the way to school, while I had a lovely big top and I used to whip this along the pavement. Every night I used to chalk a different pattern on the top while sitting in front of the large range.

There was one very cold winter when we had thirteen weeks of snow and ice. Mum had been given some old velvet curtains, and as she had been a dressmaker before she married, she made us each a coat of about three thickness of curtaining. She also managed to buy us each a pair of boys' lace up boots and while Arthur did not mind wearing these, I certainly did. I remember we used to go to the swimming baths with the school once a month, and at the time I was the only girl clumping on the white tiles in great big boots. The Yorkshire children did not seem to feel the cold, and used to wear ordinary shoes with long socks. Oh, how I hated those boots !

When the summer came, Mum said we would all go and pick blackberries, so she prepared a picnic and her basket to put them in, and off we went on a train to Shipley Glen. However, although it was fine and sunny, we did not find a single blackberry, although we found thousands of green ones. "Eee, bah gum, Missis. You must not expect to find blackberries here until October!", Mum was told and, of course, we were blackberrying on August Bank Holiday. This episode was the only thing that Mum ever talked about once we were back home in Jersey, and I think both she and Dad blotted out the war from their memories.

My paternal grandparents lived in the Isle of Wight during the war and my grandfather – who had been a gunner in the First World War – taught his trade to the new Royal Navy recruits in Portsmouth. He was a Chief Petty Officer and for a little while his eldest son, Denis, also in the Royal Navy and a CPO, was in the same barracks as him. All my uncles were in the forces; Fred and Gerald in the Royal Navy, Gordon under Montgomery and Vincent a navigator in the RAF. Unfortunately, he was reported "missing, presumed dead" fairly early in the war; his name is shown on both the St. Helier and St. Saviour's Rolls of honour.

For the summer holidays in 1942 to 1944 Mum and Dad packed a small suitcase and delivered Arthur and me to the train station in Bradford. We would be put on a train for London and they would ask the people in the carriage if they would kindly look after us until we arrived since our 'Auntie Peggy' would be picking us up in London. We would stay with Auntie Peggy overnight then she would put us on another train, this time to Portsmouth, where Grandpa would meet us and put us on the paddle steamer to Ryde where Grandma and Mary would meet us at the end of our long adventurous journey.

Although we both had a book to read (one of my favourites was Barbar the Elephant) very little reading was done as the people in the carriage used to play 'I spy', 'I went to Market and bought…' and 'The Parson's Cat'. After the war these games were always played by us at Christmas, and indeed when my own children were growing up they were all taught them, and now with my grandchildren, they are still being played at Christmas.

Once we were in the Isle of Wight we went down to Bembridge to see the lifeboat which was rolled down a steep ramp straight into the water whenever it was needed. Grandma had a huge garden and we could play hide and seek all day long. Dad's youngest sister, Mary, was only nine years older than me, and she used to invent all kinds of outdoor games for us to play. Of course, later on she had to go out to work but she still helped look after us. One holiday my father's brothers, who were in the forces, all came down to see their mother, and it was lovely for us to see our uncles. After we had been there a fortnight, Mum and Dad would come down for their holiday and we would all return to Eccleshill together.

I can remember once when the whole family was there, that I was woken up and going into the kitchen found everyone looking up into the sky listening to hundreds of our planes flying over on a bombing raid. This must have been a bittersweet moment for my grandmother, as her youngest son, Vincent, was killed on a raid and as far as I know his body was never recovered. I am so proud when I visit both St Saviour's Parish Hall and the Town Hall to see his name there on their Rolls of Honour.

As a chapel was the closest church to our house in Eccleshill, Arthur and I used to go there to Sunday School and, of course, like all chapels, they would have a Harvest Festival. I do not know how she did it, but Mum managed to get two bunches of carrots – neither of them very big. As you can probably guess, by the time we reached chapel only the green stems were left, while the carrots had been eaten and enjoyed by us on the walk there. We did get a telling off that time!

On 9 May 1945, my parents were very excited because they had heard Winston Churchill saying those immortal words ....."and our dear Channel Islands are also be freed to-day". Mum ironed an old white pillowcase, and sewed a red cross on it, before it was fixed to the broom handle and pushed out of the bedroom sash window. She spent a lot of time that day answering the front door and telling people why it was there.

In July 1945, there was a General Election in England, and to my parents' horror Mr. Churchill was defeated and the Labour Party gained an overwhelming majority. During the campaign, there were lots of meetings at my father's factory, and more than once he came home with blood on his face from blows he received from Labour supporters. I remember Mum asking him why he went to the meetings when he knew he would probably get hurt.

I passed my 11 plus exam for grammar school in the summer term of 1945, and even went for an interview but, of course, by then the war had ended and Dad was trying to get us back home to Jersey. I do not know exactly when we came home during August, but do remember Mum saying to us as we crossed St Aubin's Bay, "Do you see that house with the green roof. We live in a road just behind it." That house is still visible and every time I travel by sea I look at it and remember those words.

Once home, we had to stay at Modderfield for a while as our home was occupied by a lady and her daughter, but certainly we were living there by the time I went to the Intermediate that September for a year to learn some French before finally going to the Girls College.

Elizabeth and Arthur Fry pictured on arrival at Weymouth. Printed in the News of the World, 30th June 1940 and reproduced by their kind permission.

THE WAR EXPERIENCES OF JEAN MCLAUGHLIN née Quenault

My name is Jean McLaughlin and I am going to tell of my experiences in as much detail as I can remember as a child during the Second World War and in particular as an evacuee who left Jersey with my Mum and Dad.

I was born at 11 Belmont Gardens, Belmont Road in St Helier. My mother was Amelia Marie née Cotillard and was the eldest of nine children. My Dad's name was John Edward Quénault and he came from a family of five. In those days large families were very common.

My dad worked at Huelin's at Five Oaks making bricks. It was a very hard job and since only flimsy gloves were provided that never used to last, I remember him coming home with his hands burnt on numerous occasions. Unfortunately back then jobs were very hard to come by and so he carried on regardless of the pain and discomfort. We lived in a little cottage in Seaton Place and my mother stayed at home and looked after me. Life was very hard and it was a blessing that we survived as a family as everybody worked hard.

I was only two when the war broke out and both my Mum and Dad were worried about the Germans taking over the Island. It was a choice whether you stayed or left and both my parents decided that it would be better for me to leave our beloved Island as they had heard terrible things that the Germans did and they also didn't want to be under German rule. Looking back now it was a great decision they had had to take.

My Dad was 19 and my Mum was 21 and both had never left the Island before. I recall them being very worried. My Granny did tell my Mum to leave me with her but my parents didn't want to as I was their only child whom they adored.

I think they had to go to the Town Hall and register to leave. There were thousands of people and huge queues and we had to wait for hours. We eventually left on a coal boat called the Archangel and we were crowded aboard like cattle. I remember my Mum and Dad had to leave all their possessions and take either a carrier bag or a small case and what they stood up in with them. It must have been awful having to leave all your worldly possessions, family and friends. There were plenty of tears and hugs as you never knew when you would be returning or if you ever would. What a huge decision for them to make.

We landed in Weymouth 16 hours later. It was a long and very frightening journey. I don't remember much of the journey as I must have fallen asleep.

When we arrived in Weymouth, Winston Churchill was asking the Channel Islanders to join the forces. My Dad joined up in the hope he would be helping his island and his country but also wondered if he would ever return to his family. Many people joined up, some even lying about their ages.

In those days because we left the Island we were branded "Rats and Rabbits" for leaving a sinking ship. It was harsh and as we were barely on the boats those remaining were ransacking our houses, taking all our belongings. I presume this happens when you are in a war but we did hope we would be returning.

My Dad was in the the Dorset Regiment, part of the 14th Army, and had to do his training in different parts of the country so he found rooms for my Mum and me so we could live close to the barracks. Then came the day that my Mum was dreading; my Dad was told that he was being sent to Burma, India and the Far East to fight the Japanese and he was going to have to leave us for an indefinite period. I remember my Mum crying continuously and it being a very sad day. Dad found us a room in Weymouth. It was with an elderly lady - I can't remember her name - but we lived there for six years until my Dad returned. The house had a small garden which was by the gas works and next to a railway. The day my Dad left to go to war we went to say good-bye. I remember him picking me up, squeezing me and flooding me with kisses. My Mum was devastated and they hugged and kissed each other for ages.

When I was older my Dad told me that when he left England he could see the white cliffs of Dover getting smaller and smaller and thinking to himself 'what have I done?'. He was going to a strange country, thousands of miles away. Would he ever return to his young wife and child and to his beautiful island of Jersey? I think the journey lasted for six to eight weeks. What must these men have had to go through? They left as boys but certainly returned as men.

My Mum sent me to a school not far from where we lived and I stayed there until I was eight years old. During the five long years of war I remember my mum getting a job cleaning a public house. The people were very nice and good to her; they had a little boy whom I used to play with and we became great friends. My mum was always there for me - she used to pick me up from school and would never leave me on my own. She was a kind loving mother, I thought she was the best in the whole world. We were devoted to each other and loved each other very much.

I remember the air raid shelters, the bombings, barrage balloons which deterred the German planes, search-lights, the blackouts, barbed wire along the beaches, Mickey Mouse gas masks, ration books, powdered eggs, bottles of thick orange squash and the malt my mother used to give me to build my bones and help me to grow. Due to the lack of nourishment I used to get boils on my knees, whitlows on my thumbs and all the usual children's aliments including whooping cough, measles and chicken pox. I didn't know what a fresh egg looked like until after the war! My mother did the best she could under the circumstances; she used to save the sweet coupons and buy something that we really needed.

A Jersey Society was formed and this was where the Jersey people met every so often. It was a good thing as it brought everyone together and made everybody feel like family. I remember there being a Christmas party every year and everyone wearing Jersey badges with pride to commemorate where we came from.

We didn't have many toys in those days. My mum's friend knitted me an elephant which I adored and a lovely gollywog with blue trousers and a red jacket. I treasured these toys all through the war. I also had a black dolly and a small doll with pink knitted clothes. I felt a very lucky girl to have these toys and looked after them with a passion.

I remember one particular day while we were living in Weymouth. A German submarine, a U-boat, had been captured and it was opened to the general public could everyone could see what it was like inside. I was scared because we were actually going to see where Germans lived – they were the enemy and it really did feel odd. I held onto my mother's hand very tightly as we went inside since by now I didn't want to go in. It was so big outside yet so cramped and so very small inside. I could not believe men lived in there and travelled in it under the sea. It felt like being locked into an iron tube. I knew that I could never have lived in something like that.

101

My mum explained to me that U-boats torpedoed ships to sink them and kill the people on them; to someone of my age that seemed so terrible. It made me think how cruel war was and I was pleased that they had captured this U-boat and also the Germans who had been inside. At least there was one submarine less in the big wide ocean to continue with such destruction.

All this time Dad was fighting thousands of miles away. Sometimes we would wait for weeks and even months before we heard from him, but when a letter arrived my mum and I were overjoyed. Some of the letters had photos and it was fantastic to see his face once again. My mum used to write back and include photos of us when she could. She also used to put lipstick on our lips and we used to kiss the bottom of the letter and put our names inside the lips. This was the bond that brought us even closer together when we were all those thousands of miles apart. If ever my mum forgot to do this in the next letter Dad would write, 'Has Britain ran out of lipstick or have you not got enough coupons left?'. That lasted for the whole of the six years Dad was fighting the Japanese. What a bond we had together.

My mum did make some good friends. There was the Brewer family and Auntie Lorraine and Uncle Arthur Sausey. They had a bungalow in the country and sometimes at the weekends we used to visit. It made a lovely break as it was nice and peaceful in the country, particularly compared with living next to the gas works. Uncle Arthur used to take me with him to work in his lorry while Mum stayed with Auntie Lorraine. We were always made very welcome. They were lovely people and good friends.

I also remember the hard times, the sleepless nights with the bombing, not knowing where the bombs would land. When the bombing started we had to go down into the shelters and I remember them being very cold and having to huddle together to keep warm. We lived close to the gas works and the Germans were always trying to bomb it. I also remember having to be very careful when school finished as the German bombers often machine-gunned the streets. Weymouth seemed to get bombed quite a lot.

One morning after the bombing, and the siren had sounded the 'All Clear', we came out of the shelter and found that the entire row of houses opposite where we lived had completely gone. I felt very lucky as we were obviously on the right side. Thank God we were in the shelter and not under the steel table that we had in the house! This sort of thing happened so frequently that enduring it came quite naturally.

As a treat my mum used to take me to the pictures. We saw Old Mother Riley, George Formby, Bud Abbott and Lou Costello and the Tarzan films. I loved going and afterwards we used to buy fish, chips and mushy peas, always ending the afternoon well. Those were the good times. I can still smell those mushy peas even after all these years.

I remember my mum used to cry quite a lot because she obviously missed Dad and all the family she had left behind. I used to continually give her cuddles and kisses to help her pain. I missed my dad too and remember kissing the photo that he had sent us as we cried together.

D-Day was a memorable day. There was a curfew and you couldn't have your lights on after a certain time due to the blackout regulations but all day you also couldn't see the sky for planes and I remember looking at them out the window. My mum told me that there must be something important happening as everyone was being so quiet. Later we realised that the end of the war must be near.

Actually we didn't return to Jersey until one year later after the war was won and the Channel Islands had been liberated. Dad was still fighting as one of the 'Forgotten Army' so my mum didn't want to return without him, even though she was desperate to see her mother, brothers, sisters and friends. The day Dad came back was the most fantastic day of my life, a dream come true.

We eventually came back around Christmas 1945. The weather was really bad, it was pouring with rain, blowing a gale and the sea was rough. Just as we were coming through the pierheads we saw a man standing there wearing a cap, smoking a cigarette and looking wet through. Dad told me that it was Granddad. I was really surprised since I couldn't believe I had a granddad.

Once we docked Mum and Dad's eyes lit up as all the family had arrived to greet us. Everyone was hugging each other and I remember thinking that I now had a real family. I shall never forget that moment as long as I live - it was the most wonderful experience.

Getting back to normal life was very difficult as we had arrived back with as much luggage as we had left with six years earlier. Dad had to find a job and somewhere for us to live. We did eventually move in with Granny until Dad found a flat in Dorset Street. It was quite small with only two bedrooms, one living room and a small kitchen. There was no electric lighting so we had to use gas mantles. We stayed there until we were lucky to get a flat from the Housing Department and went to live at Pré de Talbot.

It was very hard for Mum and Dad to adjust to normal life

Dad went back to Huelin's and Mum stayed at home to look after me. However Dad was very ill for he was only six stone when he returned from India after being demobbed from the Army. I suppose he was ill because he wasn't used to eating normal food and it could have been too strong for his stomach. Life was very hard for him as he used to have nightmares of his time fighting the Japanese in the jungle where he had caught dysentery twice.

It was fantastic being a family again but it did take a long time for Dad to get better. I thank God that he ever returned to us at all; we were so lucky.

Being an evacuee was quite an existence as we had to adjust so much and so quickly to a different lifestyle. This is probably why I eat everything and never waste food because I know what it was like to be hungry. Nowadays I help people quite a lot because in those days so many people helped each other. This was the way I was brought up and this will stay with me for the rest of my life. I am very thankful to Mum and Dad for being wonderful parents and bringing me up the way they did in very difficult circumstances.

I thank you both for the good times and the precious years we all spent together as a family before and after the war. To me they were the best parents in the whole wide world and I was so very lucky to have them.

God bless you both, from your devoted and loving daughter Jean.

XXX

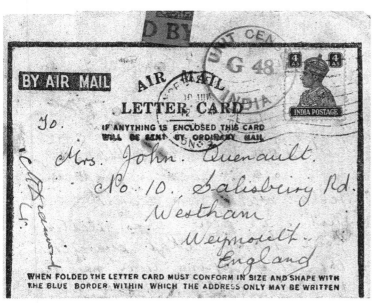

BY AIR MAIL

AIR MAIL
LETTER CARD
IF ANYTHING IS ENCLOSED THIS CARD
WILL BE SENT BY ORDINARY MAIL

To.

Mrs. John. Quenault.
No. 10., Salisbury Rd.
Westham
Weymouth.
England

WHEN FOLDED THE LETTER CARD MUST CONFORM IN SIZE AND SHAPE WITH
THE BLUE BORDER WITHIN WHICH THE ADDRESS ONLY MAY BE WRITTEN

Dear Dad, how much I miss you
'Tis very hard to say,
I think of you each morning
Each night for you I pray,
I wish you God's protection,
And surely He will care,
He knows how much I love you
And He is with you there.

Ever in
our Thoughts

A very special birthday card

Jean McLaughlin (2) with her parents just before her father went to war, 1940

née
Jean Quenault

Jean McLaughlin (8) with her parents on her father's return from the War. 1946

THE MEMORIES OF THE LATE EUPHIE LE CORNU

When we heard the guns firing in France we began to wonder how safe Jersey or the other Channel Islands would be. Then the little boats in Jersey were sent over to St Malo to evacuate the soldiers to bigger ships lying further out. This was done very quietly – we only knew about it as my husband Arthur had to get his boss's boat ready for the journey to and from St Malo.

There was some panic when we knew that the Germans were likely to land in Jersey but were told to go and register at the Town Hall if we wanted to be evacuated and I spent one afternoon standing in a queue waiting to register. We decided we could do more good and help the war effort if we left. It was hard to leave our home and all our goods.

Next day some cargo boats came into the harbour and we prepared to leave. We were only allowed to take one small case each so we left most of our things behind, taking just a few clothes.

I asked a neighbour who was staying behind to look after our cat. We had to abandon Arthur's Austin Seven and we heard later that someone had set it on fire.

I made some sandwiches and we went down to the harbour, not knowing what would happen to our house and furniture.

The people supervising the loading of the boats were not bothered about whether we had registered or not. We got on a cargo boat with metal decks.

The crew gave up their quarters to mothers with babies and young children. Most of the passengers went down in the hold but we did not fancy that and stayed on deck.

While we were waiting to board someone on the quay side was shouting that there were U-boats outside waiting to sink the ships leaving but on board everyone was quiet.

It took us nearly two days to cross. Luckily the weather was good but the iron decks were hard to sit on. Most people had taken some food with them but had been expecting the journey to last no more than 8 or 9 hours.

The crew made us some tea – real seaman's tea – the tea leaves and condensed milk put in the kettle. Then they gave us a ship's biscuit which you could only gnaw at and it lasts for hours. They look like those large square dog biscuits and they stop you from feeling too hungry. Some mothers had not brought enough baby food for two days but those that had plenty shared theirs.

I don't know how far down the Channel we went but it took us a long time. At one point we had a shot fired across our bows and a Royal Navy corvette came rushing up to tell us we were going into a mine field.

The boat Edwin Cabot was on did go onto a minefield at night and they were told not to move till daylight and wait till a naval vessel came to guide them off. Those on board can't have enjoyed that night much.

The afternoon of the second day we docked at Weymouth where there were military people waiting. Any man of call up age who was not a Jerseyman was taken off to join one of the forces. That was hard on their wives and children.

Jerseymen could not be called up until they had lived on the mainland for two years. We were taken to a school and given some stew and then had to sleep on some straw on the floor. Next day those that had somewhere to go were given travel passes and we went up to my relatives in Ellesmere.

Arthur found work at a R.A.F. maintenance unit and for a while we stayed with my relatives – but they also had soldiers billeted on them. So we eventually moved to a little cottage nearer Arthur's work. The cottage had no running water, no drains, no gas or electricity. There was a pump in the back garden and the nearest town was nearly three miles away.

Arthur worked long hours, leaving home around 6.00 am and sometimes it would be 10.00 pm before he returned and was often working a seven day week. If a plane was wanted in a hurry the men just had to keep working till it was ready. I remember one night it had been snowing hard and travel was bad and Arthur did not come home and I did not know whether he was working or stuck in a snowdrift. No telephones then to find out.

We had some very cold winters then and many of the planes were parked around fields and under hedges in case of bombs but it was very cold working on those planes.

I know that many of those who stayed behind regarded those who left as cowards but the great majority worked hard and none had it easy. Our neighbour in Jersey joined the Fire Service in London and was out fighting fires right through the 'blitz', enduring all that bombing. At least back in Jersey nobody was dropping bombs on you!

THE MEMORIES OF YVONNE TORPY née LE MASURIER

Before we left Jersey we were living at St Aubin in the bungalow that is now The Shell House at Seven Oaks.

My father took us down to the boat. There was a policeman down there and when we were saying goodbye he told my father to get on the boat with us. Our aunt and uncle and their two female children and Grandma came as well, so we had the captain's cabin.

I was seven years old on 28 June 1940 so I did not remember a lot.

We got on a train to Knowsley Station, then we all had to be taken to a dance hall in Bury. There were people with houses for all of us. The former mayor chose us for his new house in Chesham Fold Estate. We lived at 26 Chaffinch Drive. The cement on the doorstep was still wet!

The table was laid for us for tea and the larder was full of food. The fire was lit and there was coal in the coal hole so we were lucky.

Aunty, uncle and the girls lived in Goldfinch Drive in the same estate.

I remember one day a doodlebug flew over and then the engine stopped. We knew that meant it was going to fall nearby and it actually landed about a mile away in the grounds of Dainsmor Children's Home where some Guernsey children lived. I do not think anyone was hurt.

I remember the Manchester blitz when all the sky was lit up.

My father was a decorator and he had a job painting cinemas. He was working all the week in different places like Bolton and Blackburn, only coming home at weekends.

We went to Eastward Junior School and Senior School and later my sister went to Bury High School. Our two brothers were working when we left Bury, one was a printer and the other was in a music shop.

I remember we had ration books. My mother sent us down to the shop to get some eggs and we were allowed three eggs for seven of us. I had them in my pocket and when I pushed the gate open I squashed the eggs! My mother wasn't pleased.

We had another sister born in Bury in 1944, two years after my younger sister. We used to call her baby Irene. She was just one year old when we came back to Jersey.

When we returned my father had his job back with Mr Boneyface the builder in St Aubin. Mr Boneyface was working in a house on the Bulwarks in St Aubin which he said was for sale so we lived there. At first we had a shop then we opened a guest house. I was eighteen years old when my mother died, so I had to cook for fourteen guests.

My older brother, his wife and daughter emigrated to New Zealand. My father decided, a few years later, to sell the guest house. My older sister went to London to get married and my father decided to go to New Zealand with my two younger sisters. I did not want to go so I got a job living in with Mr and Mrs Harrison and Sally for four years, until I got married.

My other brother gave me away and then they to emigrated to New Zealand with four children and had another four girls out there. I have not seen them for 48 years although my two sisters and oldest brother did come back to Jersey just the once.

.

THE MEMORIES OF GEORGE SYMONS

My name is George Symons. I was born on 26 April 1935 and I'm a twin and my brother's name is David. We left Jersey in June 1940 when we were five years old with our parents, Charles and Alice Symons, and went to Weymouth. From Weymouth we went up to Finchley, in London. During the boat journey my twin brother and I were taken ill, and when we got to Weymouth the Red Cross took us over, cleaned us up and gave everybody cups of tea and things like that, and then made sure we were on the right transport to Finchley where my parents' cousins lived.

We stayed in Finchley for a fortnight and while we were there my parents signed up to join the forces. My father joined the army and my mother the ATS. My brother and I were signed up for a school in Penzance in Cornwall and once my parents went into the services we were transported there by train.

We were taken to Paddington Station by one of our cousins. The station was a collecting point for the school. The train made lots of stops en route to Penzance and at each stop we were expecting to get off, by the time we had had a fifth stop, then a sixth stop and then a seventh, we began to wonder what was going on. After all we were only five years of age.

On the train we were looked after by carers from the school who were complete strangers. We were the last to get off but because we were twins we were not to be separated. What's more we were identical twins and they only way they could tell us apart was because one of us had a G on his case and the other had a D, and we both had our initials on our jumpers. We were taken from the station to a church hall in Porthleven and the villagers in that village came round and selected the children they wanted.

However because we couldn't be separated we were the last to be chosen and the people who took us happened to be passing by and saw us there, two little kiddies and said they would take us in. They had no children of their own and they took us in because their surname was the same as ours, Symons, spelt exactly the same way, although we were not related in any way. Harold and Olive were our foster parents and they turned out to be a wonderful couple. During the five years we were there they treated us like their own sons. In those five years we only saw our father three times and our mother once. The people who took us in also took in injured service personnel to convalesce after leaving hospital. They were all in uniforms and when my parents came down, when they did manage to come down, they were in uniform too. We didn't know they were our family, because we were only six years of age and because our name was Symons and we were living with people called Symons, we were a little bit confused. For five years they looked after us very well down there, and they were good people.

The worst part had been from the time we left the Jersey to the time we arrived in Cornwall. Having left a peaceful island all we experienced was hustle, bustle and strange people in different costumes and uniforms. We were so confused and at times very scared but we couldn't turn round and say we didn't want to go or we didn't feel well, things like that, because we had nobody we knew to turn to.

It was hard going, but we settled in and the villagers accepted us. There were only about six evacuees down there from different parts of the country and they treated us evacuees very well. The place we went to was Porthleven, two and a half miles from Helston, a very picturesque place, a nice little fishing village, and a mile up the road was the countryside, very nice.

We had a British Bren gun carrier squadron down there. They didn't have much in the way of sweets or chocolate or anything, but they treated us well. Then they pulled out and the Americans arrived. As far as we, the evacuees, and the village people were concerned they were foreigners who lived thousands of miles away. The young ladies of the village were very happy to see them; they had everything, sweets, chocolate, fruit juices and things like that. When they heard there were evacuees in the village, the Colonel decided to have a party for them. He said that his American troops were a thousand miles away from home and they could appreciate what the evacuees had gone through. So the Americans treated us very well. The people, that generation of people, were wonderful.

The hardest part was leaving after five years. We left our foster parents who took us on a train to Penzance and put us on another train that took us all the way back to Paddington and after five years that was the hardest thing.

The only thing I could remember on the way up from Penzance to Paddington was all the damaged buildings. In that area they were trying to hit Falmouth docks, they were hitting Plymouth and there was a military airport about two and a half miles away and they were trying to hit that too. All that long trip I realised how much damage had been done.

Then it was back to Finchley again with our cousins and I don't know how long we were there but we came back to Jersey in September 1945, and stayed with an aunt until we found a place to live in Clare Street, next to Randall's Brewery. It took a long time to settle down again.

When our parents returned they were strangers and we didn't recognise them. As far as my brother and I were concerned we had to start again, a new life. It was hard for we had to have a new routine. The trouble is I get so upset because I can still remember saying goodbye to my foster parents.

Roughly that's the story. We had good times, don't get me wrong, as two little boys almost on our own.

After the war and after we had settled back in Jersey, we did go back about every two years to see those foster parents, and later took our wives over to meet everyone. We were the only evacuees who returned to visit our foster parents. The villagers used to say, "Here's the twins again." They hadn't forgotten us!

Charles and Alice Symons with twins David and George in 1942

113

THE MEMORIES OF SHIRLEY SYMONS née BARRY

My name is Shirley Symons (nee Barry), I was born on 20 February 1937 and I was an evacuee.

Based on what my parents, James & Ethel (Sue) Barry told me, like everybody else I suppose, they heard so many rumours that the Germans were coming and they would take all the children away, etc. that panic set in.

It was all rumours.

They queued all day for tickets to get on the boat and in those days you just boarded the boat as it arrived. So on 20 June 1940 we found ourselves in the hold of a cargo boat setting out for Weymouth. It took 14 hours to get there due to mines at the harbour mouth and when we finally disembarked we were given drinks and biscuits.

We were put onto a train to Bolton, where we were housed in a school hall for six weeks. My brother Sidney was only three months old at the time and as we were allocated one camp bed per family, we two children slept in the bed and my mother slept in a chair. They were trying to find different billets to put people in and my mother always said it was just like a cattle market. People used to come along and look you up and down to see if they wanted to take you into their home. Some of them wanted my brother because he was a baby, but my mother wanted to keep us together. Luckily my father came with us as well, but he went off to find work and he managed to find somewhere in Bolton that had a live-in position as a barman.

We were one of the last group of families left with young children and Bury Council eventually offered to allocate houses that had just been finished to Channel Islanders. So around fifty Guernsey and Jersey families went to live in Bury. My father was still working in Bolton and it was six weeks before he knew were we had moved to. There had been no way of letting him know since we had left by tram for Bury at such short notice.

When we arrived in Bury because the houses had only just been built and so they were empty and Bury Council, the WVS and a lot of other people all helped to furnish them. There was always tinned milk and things like that to start us off. Of course nobody knew we were going to be there for five years and we had bare boards upstairs because we didn't have the facilities or the finances to get things like mats and carpets. We didn't know how long we were going to be there. My brother Douglas was born in 1942 in Bury and it was lovely helping to look after him.

Bury is in Lancashire, and we were 10 miles from Bolton. There were quite a few families there, and it was lovely. I just remember going to school, St Joseph's Catholic School, and things like that. My father joined the Fire Service as did a lot of the Channel Islands men. He often said how strange it was being told to take a fire tender to a certain place, and because he had never ever been away from Jersey, didn't have a clue where any place was. There were no signs - they all had to be taken down because of the war, so it was often the case of stopping every few miles and asking the way. He also went to Plymouth after the bombing. The city was gutted and he was there six weeks, then to Manchester when that city was badly bombed. He was always out and about, moving all the time. Every time there was a big bombing raid anywhere, he was there. He got injured once. In Bury there was a drill hall where they used to keep all the equipment and ammunition for the Home Guard, and it caught fire. There were explosions and he got badly injured while fighting the fires. It was very hard for them.

The only thing I used to enjoy was the winters, the snow was fantastic up there, it was so deep, but we still had to go to school and it was hard going as it was quite a long way to walk.

People left in Jersey thought we were cowards for running away. They just thought it was going to be like a holiday but, of course, we had to endure all the bombing. I used to be terrified when the air raid sirens went off, because you never knew what would happen and we were waiting to hear that noise come over. We always had to go downstairs, take our pillows with us and get under a big table. There weren't any air raid shelters where we were staying. They started building one but it never got finished. At school as well, we always had to have these gas masks with us every time we left home. It was horrible because we had to practice going down into an air raid shelter which was in the middle of the playground. I remember it was always wet and smelt awful down below ground, but we got through it.

We were severely rationed, we had to have ration books and clothing coupons, which must have been very hard for parents, but as a child we just enjoyed things, as children do. Our grandmother Louise St George and my two Aunts Linda and Florence who were both teenagers, were also evacuated to Bolton, so we used to visit them occasionally on the trams.

There was a Channel Islands Society. My father and a lot of the other men formed Jersey and Guernsey teams and used to play football. It was just like the annual inter-island Muratti. They used to try and do it every year and that was good. Then they put on concerts and everybody would sing and do plays, we dressed in red and white, for Jersey, and they dressed in green and white for Guernsey. I remember going round singing with a few of the children. We used to visit Bolton, Manchester and Rochdale, all that area, and go to all of the other societies there. We linked up with the other people and they used to come to us as well. So there were a lot of good things going on, the societies used to get together and we used to have a party, especially towards the end of the war. We even went on a day trip to Blackpool kindly organised by the Mayor of Bury.

The most horrible thing was always having to take those gas masks everywhere, although they were in little boxes, you always had to have them with you. And it was the air raid sirens mostly that were really frightening. Also, I hated wearing clogs, but they lasted very well.

We lived on the outskirts of Bury, the country part, and were quite high up so you could see the red in the sky when Manchester was burning, and I can remember my mother calling us to see it, when it happened. We lived near woods and a farm so we had plenty of open spaces to play in.

We didn't come back until November 1945, because you had to wait for the billet lady to come along and tell you when you could go back to Jersey on the boat. If you wanted to go back you had to have a job to go to and a home. Our home when we left had only been a little cottage and it was completely gutted, people had taken all the stuff out of it. My aunt lived just round the corner and the day after we had left she went round to see if she could collect some of our things, but everything was gone. It could only have been neighbours that took it, because nobody else knew we had gone. It is the same now, when there are floods and suchlike people won't leave their homes because they think their possessions are going to be taken.

People wouldn't leave, because they knew all their stuff would be taken, and that's how it was when we came back, on 5 November. Luckily an aunt had returned before us and she managed to get the same cottage back, in Clairvale Road, because the landlady had said she would try and keep it for us. When we got back there, there was nothing in the house and my father would go round second-hand sales to try and furnish it. So it was really hard for the parents, how they coped was great, they worried what was happening to the families back home in Jersey.

My father used to work at RM Stores in King Street before the war and returned there when we came back. But he was treated very badly, being called a 'rabbit' and a 'rat' for running away. Some of his workmates were really awful, they were the ones that probably looted our possessions!

I think my Mother was very reserved, a very quiet person, and because we left a home to go to England, made another home there and then had to leave and start all over again, she never wanted to go on holiday, and never was one for going out. I'm sure she thought that if she went away, she would lose her home. It's understandable when you think about it. A lot of people stayed in Bury as they had jobs and homes.

Sidney (3), Douglas (1) and Shirley (6) Barry in 1943

A Muratti football team before playing in February 1942 in Bury, Lancs.
Guernseyman C. Coyde was accepted as a Reserve

Back row : left to right -
C. Coyde, J. Barter, T. Noel, C. Cornick, E. Belhomme,
B. Champion, J. Barry

Sitting : R. Le Signe, W. Sayce, C. Gioty, L. de la Mare, H.Belhomme

Back row : far left - Reserve J. Harrison
Back row : far right - Jack Roche, later Constable and Deputy of St
Saviour

THE MEMORIES OF JEAN VENABLES

My grandparents were the proprietors of the La Pulente Hotel before the war. My mother, father, aunts and uncles all helped out with the running of the hotel. When they eventually got tickets for the passage there were twelve people plus one - a good family friend and a "general help allsorts". Of these thirteen, three were children, one being my brother William who was seven years old at the time.

My mother told me many tales of that two day journey, the boat having to go at low speed due to mines. Mother said they were all hungry and thirsty as the boat was not equipped to deal with so many passengers.

Cousin Peter, a babe in arms, was put in a drawer in the Captain's quarters to sleep.

Apparently a lady dressed completely in white sat under the funnel and certainly was not pristine white after two days!

The Captain brought out a tin of ship's biscuits and one poor chap was so hungry he shoved his hand into the tin and cut his hand on the jagged lid.

On reaching the end of the boat journey the only people who greeted them were the wonderful Salvation Army. My father was so dehydrated he had thirteen cups of tea!

They made for South Wales as we had family there and my wonderful great aunt Gert put all of them up until they found accommodation. I was born two years later on 6 June 1941.

My grandfather Mr E Williams had left his car on the pier. The dogs were kept by my one aunt who stayed in Jersey for the duration. As they had left the hotel all silver, linen and everything was ransacked by neighbours and, of course, subsequently the La Pulente Hotel was ruined. My grandfather was contacted at the end of the war to renew his proprietorship but he felt too old to start all over again.

Eight of us came to live in Jersey as my father and uncle were offered their old jobs back.

My grandfather had fought in the Boer war. My father and one of my uncles had been in the Army. In fact my grandfather was catering manager at the old St Peter's Barracks near the airport before taking on La Pulente Hotel.

119

THE EVACUEE SCHOOLBOY'S STORY OF ANTHONY TROY

I was born Anthony Alan Troy, forever after known as Tony. Although I have been called other names but we won't go into that! I was four years old when we evacuated to England, all the signs were in French as the English people thought that was all we could speak. Most could not understand what the notices said.

Channel Islanders were sent to different parts of England. We were sent up north to Lancashire and lived in Bury at 112 Fern Grove. The street names in our area were named after flora or birds and most of the houses were supposed to be for evacuees from Holland, which never happened.

My father, the late John Troy, known by everyone as Jack, was too old to serve in the forces. He had been in the Royal Flying Corps, later to become the R.A.F., in the first World War.

The Channel Islands Association was set up and the Lord Mayor of Manchester was President, Lady Knott of Samarès was Vice President and my father, Jack Troy, was Chairman. In addition to assisting C.I. families in distress the Society circulated news of births, marriages and deaths of Channel Islanders that had taken place in England or had been received in Red Cross messages from the Island.

I remember one young Jerseyman, Jack Duhamel, coming to speak to my father for advice. He had left Jersey on his own, following his elder brother Gerald who had joined the Navy, but Gerald had split on him that he was under age. He did eventually join the Navy. Both brothers did survive the war although not with us today. Little did I know that in 1956 I would marry their youngest sister Sylvia – well, they do say it's a small world.

The news of the forming of the Association was received in Jersey by my father's brother, the late Richard Troy, and reported in the The Evening Post of the time, and again repeated in the column under "25 years ago".

At the end of the war my father was presented with a large brass carriage clock in appreciation for what he had done with the inscription:

Presented to Mr John Troy
Chairman of the Bury and District
Channel Islands Association
1940-1945

My father worked very closely with a Mr John Fletcher, a retired commercial traveler, who took the Channel Islanders to his heart and organized many events and outings for them.

At the end of the war when we had returned to Jersey, my father brought John Fletcher over to Jersey to meet all those he had befriended and to see our Island. We all met in Coronation Gardens at Millbrook one evening. This was reported in The Evening Post of the time.

My eldest brother Edward, known to us as Ted, worked for a time in the Post Office, later joining the 7th Airborne Division, known to the Germans as the Red Devils, because of their maroon berets. He was dropped over Germany then sent on to Palestine via Malta. He was a lucky one to come back, and today we still have unrest in Palestine.

My only sister Nancy worked for a time in Bensons sweet factory and in a shoe factory. Being the only girl in the family she was a great companion and helper for my mother.

My second eldest brother was John, the same name as my father, there being six years difference between John and Ted and five years between John and myself, Nancy being five years older than John. He seemed to be more of a loner; we would try to get home from school before him to use his bogey (go cart). We also made kites out of newspapers and a little flour and water, like the rest of the Channel Islanders we made the most of what we had. John would help the milkman deliver the milk around with the horse and cart, one night a bomb dropped on the farm and did a lot of damage and the glass fell out of our back window.

The rag and bone man would come around occasionally with his horse and cart (no cars in those days) and my mother would try to find a few rags to get a donkey stone (pumice stone) or a windmill, a stick with cellophane propeller to keep us quiet.

We first went to Eastward School. My mother Gladys took myself and two younger brothers Colin and Brian to school and back every day. My first teacher was Miss Marsh, I cannot remember any of the other teachers' names. She was a horror: I'm sure she is burning in Hell! Eastward was not a Catholic school and since we were going to church every Sunday, it was not long before the old priest was around the house telling my mother we should be going to St. Joseph's School and learning our catechism. She disagreed and sent him packing, telling him St Joseph's was too rough.

Shortly afterwards a younger priest came to the house and with a softer approach persuaded my mother to send us to St Joseph's Catholic School, promising her we would not be caned. The promise was not kept.

I think the Headmaster must have been a bit sadistic for I had the cane or strap on hand or backside nearly every day just for being late while my mother took us to school. My two younger brothers used to be taken to the kindergarten part of the school first. However I never told my mother about the caning in case she made a fuss.

The District Nurse was visiting everyone and tonsils were coming out everywhere. When she visited us, shoving a spoon half way down our throats, she told our mother that we three young ones had to go to hospital and have our tonsils out. My mother said she would get a second opinion from a doctor and had to tell her in no uncertain manner to leave. We did see a doctor and the three of us still have our tonsils. My mother was five foot nothing but no one ordered her about.

We would go and play sometimes in an old ruin, sliding down the sloping floor, and one day I found a thick piece of yellow glass. I took it home and gave it to my mother telling her it might be a diamond (silly boy). My mother kept it for more than 60 years giving it back to me a couple of years before she died. I still have it and treasure it.

The King and Queen came to Bury at the end of the war and someone thought it would be a good idea to set the rubber dump down the road (or down yonder, as the Lancashire people would say) from our house on fire to celebrate the occasion. I remember the flames rising high in the sky together with huge black clouds of smoke. I ran home saying my prayers, I had never seen such a large fire.

When looking back and thinking about the evacuees, times must have been much harder for the parents since children can adapt much more easily. My father had been a successful businessman and ended up in England with his family and nothing else. Like many others on his return to Jersey he started all over again and built up a successful business.

On returning to Jersey we were met by my father's brother Bob and my mother's sister, Mrs May Glover, and her daughter Tiny. There was lots of hugging and tears. God bless them all.

THE MEMORIES OF VERONICA OLGA EDWARDS
Formerly Du Feu, née Lozach

My name is Veronica Olga Edwards, formerly du Feu, née Lozach. I was evacuated from Jersey on the 20 June 1940 with my son Ronald. My husband Ronald du Feu was in the Jersey Militia and was on board a ship, ready to sail to England. We said our goodbyes at the dock.

I went to see my father who lived at La Croix au Maitre to tell him that I was leaving for England. With my son, I boarded a cargo boat and that night we slept on bare boards in the hold. This boat must have been used to carry oranges because I can still remember the overpowering smell! In the morning seamen brought us tea in enamel mugs and hardtack biscuits.

We landed at Weymouth and were labeled up with F.F.I. labels (Free From Infection). The authorities were trying to find out where the Jersey Militia had landed. However after two or three hours I was dozing in a chair with my son, I looked up and I thought I saw my sister Gladys Faramus. I looked again, and it was her, with her husband and two small daughters. They had a shop in Kensington Place at the time. I told the authorities that I would stay with my sister. We later found out from the Red Cross that the Jersey Militia had landed at Southampton and had moved on to the Isle of Wight.

Initially, with my sister Gladys's family, we were sent to Rochdale and though the people there were very kind, it was a depressing place after our lovely Jersey. In Rochdale we heard that my youngest sister Olga was in St Helens, Lancashire, and she was planning to go to the Isle of Wight as her boyfriend Louis Le Long was stationed there. We agreed to meet up and go to the Isle of Wight.

While there I worked for a year in a ship building factory and when volunteers were called for the Forces I joined the Auxiliary Territorial Service (the A.T.S.). The lady we rented rooms from had offered to look after my son. In the A.T.S. I was a radar operator on a heavy anti-aircraft site.

On 6 March 1942 my husband Ronald Du Feu, who was from St Martin, was killed in North Africa. He was 26 years old.

I met my second husband in the Forces and we had a daughter.

My son became a bank manager and emigrated to Canada with his wife and three small children. He is now retired and has two grandchildren. My daughter is married with two children and three grandchildren.

I am in good health after a triple by-pass and aorta replacement and at 89 can still play bowls!

THE MEMORIES OF PHILIP AND DOROTHY VIVIAN
recalled by their daughter Helene

Dorothy (Dolly) & Philip (Phil) Vivian were married in January 1937 in Jersey. They first lived in a flat above what later became the Jersey Electricity Company shop in Broad Street in St Helier. Phil, who loved to drive, operated a taxi; the cab company base was just across the road from where they lived. Helene was born on 14 October 1937. Later the family moved to a very small house in Clifton Place in Ann Street. Phil changed jobs and now drove a lorry picking up milk from the farms and delivering to Tanguy's Dairy. Pat was born 4 May 1940. By this time the Second World War was underway with the Germans advancing already well into France.

In mid-June 1940, expecting the German military to move into the Channel Islands at any day soon, Phil and Dolly decided it would be best to evacuate to England. Within a few hours they got together clothing and a few necessities in a bag for the two babies. They themselves just wore their clothing. "Two of everything" as Dolly recalled. As it happened, the ship was only able to take women and children, so in what must have been an awful decision to make, they agreed that Dolly, 25, would escape on this ship to England with Helene, two and a half, and Pat, six weeks old, with the hope that Phil could follow soon.

This was not to be for the Germans arrived in Jersey during the next day or so and occupied the Islands for five years. Pat had lost a knitted bootee which Phil kept in his wallet for the entire duration of the war.

Meanwhile the refugee ship arrived safely in southern England, and this large group of people were put up in a hall for the night. The next day, some went on to relatives; Dolly and family, along with a group of others, were dispatched by train to Barnsley, a small coal mining town in Yorkshire.

At first they lived in an inadequate, dingy little room. A kind family took pity on them and invited them to move into their home until a better place could be found. This house had only two bedrooms, a kitchen, a living room and and outdoor flush toilet. They lent Dolly one bedroom, and their two little daughters slept on the sofa in the living room.

Now comes the first part of the story that I, Helene, personally remember. Dolly, my mum, looked after the children while their mother, Nellie, worked as a conductor (clippie) on the buses. Nellie's husband was a coal miner: he got his daily shower at the worksite bathhouses. We were with this family for about a year until we moved in with another refugee family in a house near Cundy Cross on the outskirts of Barnsley.

This house had three bedrooms and a full bathroom. The family consisted of father, Bob Lewis, mother Freda, daughter Jean (eighteen months younger than me) and a son Robert, born a few months after we joined them. Also there was a lovely grandmother, Granny Lewis, who did a lot of looking after and playing with the little ones. She made handicrafts with us; we made a paper chain that Christmas time, using strips of coloured pages from an old magazine and flour and water paste. She took us to Sunday School at the Wesleyan Chapel, and got us to say our prayers. I believe Bob, who was English, and Freda, who was Austrian, had been living and working during the tourist season in Jersey, so they had to flee back to England as refugees at the start of the war.

I enjoyed our 18 months in this house. Freda and Bob had the main bedroom, Granny Lewis had a small room, and we had the other bedroom. We all, Mum, Pat and I slept in a double bed, although I think Pat had a crib (cot) for a while until Robert Lewis was born. Bob was in the armed forces and away most of the time. When he came home on leave, Jean, who otherwise slept with her Mum, came in and shared our bed, with one child at the foot. This was the favourite place to sleep, so we had to take turns with it. The living room was a good size, and on miserable days weatherwise, the oddments of furniture were pushed to the sides to make a good playroom.

It was while living here we had our first news from Jersey in a Red Cross letter. The letter was only about twenty words long, all that was allowed. It told us that Dad and Mum's family were all right. This was 1942, two years since we had left. I remember well because Auntie Freda and Mum were so joyful one minute and then Mum burst into tears. It was the first time that I consciously thought about the fact that I had a Dad "a long way away over the water". It was fascinating to us that there were holes in the letter and Mum and Freda discussed what words might have been chopped out by the censor and why.

With Granny Lewis able to babysit sometimes, Mum got a little housekeeping job at a nearby house, Grange View. The people had a service station, garage and small grocery shop next to the house. As the wife was busy helping with these small businesses, someone was needed to clean house and cook lunch for a few hours two or three mornings a week. While working there Mum met her friend Sally who worked in the grocery shop. Sally was very young, still in her teens, and had just married. Her husband was a soldier and away for long periods of time. She asked Mum to come and live with her as she often felt afraid being on her own. We moved in with Sally for about a year, which was fine except when her husband came home on leave. Naturally it felt awkward and we had to stay out of the way as much as possible. However, a few houses away, at the corner of the street, an older couple, Mr and Mrs Pearce, had to move in with and care for a very elderly mother living next door to them. They asked Mum if she would occupy and look after their house for them, an excellent arrangement which lasted for about 18 months until the end of the war.

We were in school at that time, Littleworth Primary School, with Pat in the nursery so Mum was able to continue her job at Grange View, which was almost opposite where we now lived. At school the British Government supplied mid-morning milk, 1/3 pint, and cod liver oil tablets to all primary school children. Hot lunches were free to needy children, which most were with the majority of fathers away fighting the war. Lunches consisted of lots of mashed potatoes, cabbage, thin gravy with a little meat in it, and dessert, mostly prunes, occasionally stewed apple or rhubarb, and watery custard. The teachers had to make sure we ate it all too because this was the main meal of the day! That was the best that could be done at this time and ensured that children received the necessary nourishment to stay reasonably healthy, a credit to a country at war.

Refugees were given a small allowance which barely covered rent, food and heating. Mum's job helped buy shoes, and wool and fabric for making clothing. A neighbour lent Mum a hand sewing machine in return for her doing a bit of sewing and mending for them. Mum was resourceful and used an old coat she was given to make us winter coats. Odd fabric and wool leftovers were made into cloth dolls for us. Unable to sew during the long winter evenings because she could not afford to pay for the extra electricity for lighting, Mum would knit until the light became too dim then go to bed.

We could only use one of the bedrooms, and all three of us slept in one double bed. Somehow she always managed to save just a wee bit of money in case it was otherwise urgently needed.

A Jersey Refugee Group was formed to keep everyone together and help anyone in dire need. They would put on occasional amateur concerts and a children's Christmas Party. There were also local concerts put together by anyone willing to sing, dance, perform magic or comedy skits. Not having a radio, we enjoyed going to these with Mum. We were issued with gas masks early on, which we were supposed to take to school and everywhere we went at first, but we never had to use them.

One occurrence from when we were living with "Aunty Sally" in 1943 does stand out in my mind. Mum had found her Aunt Alice's address in Bournemouth by putting a notice in the newspaper. So we went for a visit at Christmas time, travelling down by train. Bournemouth being on the coast actually was a bit of a dangerous place to be at that time, but we enjoyed our week's visit. On the journey back again, the train arrived in Barnsley late at night. The last regular bus had gone, but there was a worker's bus taking men to the night shifts at the factories and coal mines. We were able to get a ride on this to the top of the road which led to Cundy Cross where we lived. We were let off the bus in pitch blackness, you couldn't even see your hand in front of your face. No lights were allowed in the total blackout; there was a skiff of snow on the ground. We had to sort of feel our way to the pavement, then go on our way down this road. Mum was aware of the curb, Pat who was three and a half was in the middle, and I had the bushes on my side. So as long as Mum felt the curbside and I the bushes, we were o.k. We must have slept on the train because I remember feeling quite wide awake, and to a six year old, this was quite an adventure. Walking along slowly, chatting away, it felt as if the road was never ending when suddenly Mum stopped, shushed us then spoke out loud. "Excuse me!" to which there was a reply from the absolute blackness: "Who are you? What are you doing here?" Mum explained our situation and enquired whether we were on the right road for Cundy Cross. The man let out a sigh of relief: "Whew!", and said we had given him quite a scare as he never met a soul on this road. We were just passing the little old chapel and would soon arrive at Cundy Cross. He was on his way to night shift work and was pushing his bike. What fascinated me so was a tiny spot of light moving around: it was the cigarette he was holding. This was the only thing we could see. I asked Mum how she knew he was there and she told me she had heard the whirring of his bicycle wheel.

Continuing on our way, we at last came to another roadway. Making our way across expecting to land just outside "Aunty Sally's" house, we found we had got to the island in the centre of the crossroads (still there in year 2000). We walked around on it, crossed the road again, only to find we were right opposite to where we were aiming for. So across the road we went again and this time found the railings and steps up to the house. Luckily it was the right one when considering all the houses along there had identical entranceways. Pat managed to knock her face on the railings and next day had a lovely black eye.

I didn't really feel afraid until the last year of the war, and then I could sense Mum's great anxiety at times, especially when hearing aircraft flying over because we were so near the steel mill towns of Sheffield and Doncaster. However, children were happy as ever together, making up games to play, skipping, hopscotch, making houses out of lines of small rocks. Also we enjoyed school. Although Barnsley was a very grimy place with the coal mines, there was a little wood nearby which in springtime was covered with beautiful bluebells and what a fantastic scent they gave out. Watercress grew in a small stream there too.

At the end of the war, May 1945, blackout curtains were taken down, street lights came on again, flags were flying. Dad sent a letter which contained a photograph of me which he had kept in his wallet throughout the war, along with Pat's baby bootee; I have that very photograph. It has a little note on the back that he wrote. He also sent a photo of himself, requested by Mum because Pat and I otherwise would not know what he looked like. He sent a bit of money to help with our fares to get back to Jersey. During the war, Mum had managed to get photos taken of us, especially for Dad and Grandma.

The day before we were to leave we went to say good bye to the lady Mum worked for, and jokingly Mum said "Would you like me to clean up the 'Bogey Hole' before I go?" Naturally I wanted to know what this was. She took us round the side of the house to where an outside door led to a small room which was not much more than a five foot square cupboard under the stairs. It was a storage room with a couple of old chairs, a table and lawnmower. But on the wall was a little cupboard which opened out to show a map of England. This room had been used as a place for possible 'underground action' meetings, had it ever been necessary. Mum's job was to make sure that odds and ends, tea mugs and cigarette butts were cleared up after meetings, and that it looked like nothing more than a storage room.

In July 1945 we returned by train to Southampton and boat to Jersey, along with a large group of people going home. The docks were crowded with family and friends meeting the loved ones they hadn't seen for five long hard years. It was so exciting to meet my grandmother and other relatives, and especially Dad. In reality these were almost strangers to Pat and me, and we had to get to know them all over again. They could hardly understand what we were saying either, with our strong Yorkshire accents; at first Mum had to translate for Dad!

We were not allowed on to the beaches for a few weeks because of possible mines. The odd mine would wash up for years afterwards and we were always warned to stay well away from any such object. By mid-August the barbed wire was removed, and it was just gorgeous to feel the old cobbled granite slipway leading to the beach, warm on our feet. The feel of the sand and playing in it, the ripples and waves at the edge of the sea, were wonderful sensations.

We started back to school in September, the little St James Street Primary, five minutes walk away. We soon fitted in, and our Yorkshire accents gradually turned round to Jersey. Because the islands were so isolated during the war, some common childhood diseases simply didn't break out. Just before Christmas that first year back, practically the whole of our school, which consisted of only 100 children, was down with chicken pox as an epidemic swept through. Pat and I had already had chicken pox in England, so we and a few others were put together to make one class for a few days.

In 1946 our sister Janet was born, and a few months later we moved to a new address, 25 Great Union Road. Our brother Derek was born in 1950. In 1954, when I was 17, I felt the need strongly to revisit Cundy Cross, near Barnsley. It struck me as extremely grimy compared to Jersey, due to the coal mines in the area. I stayed in "Auntie Sally's" house and enjoyed meeting the very kind and friendly people we had known during the war years.

When in September 2000 I visited Barnsley with my husband Mike, I didn't know quite what to expect. However, the coal mines were now shut down, the whole place had had a good facelift and generally looked great. I was thrilled to find the crossroads at Cundy Cross. The house where Mum had worked, Grange View, still had the service station next to it. I remembered our old address as soon as I read the name Grange Crescent. The house we had lived in during 1943 to 1945, No.15 Grange Crescent, along with the others which were basically the same pattern, had had new brick facings and windows put in. We also found the little Wesleyan Chapel and the Littleworth Primary School. The area was very much built up now, with houses where fields had been.

WE'RE GOING HOME - MY STORY by PAT VIVIAN

Pat Vivian, now Mrs Pat Melluish, and living in Canada, was the youngest of the evacuees. She left the Island with her mother and sister at the age of six weeks.

My mother, Dorothy Vivian, sister Hélène and I were evacuated to Barnsley, Yorkshire from Jersey in June 1940. My claim to fame is that I was apparently the youngest evacuee – just six weeks old. I think it was published in The Evening Post newspaper at the time.

My father planned to accompany us to England, but had to disembark when it was announced that it was the vessel could take women and children only.

Apparently my father had a hard time persuading my young mother (25) to go alone with two small children. My sister was only two and half years old. They tussled on the gangplank and I lost a bootee, which my father picked up and kept in his wallet all of his life. He said that the war would be over in six months!

Alone with two babies, my mother had a baggage problem when we arrived in England. She could only take what she could handle herself, so she put on as many layers of clothing as she could, and then stuffed children's things into one bag.

There are many interesting tales that my mother could tell about five years away from family, alone with two children. Fortunately, she has quite a sense of humour.

I believe she had a small allowance from Britain but supplemented her income by dressmaking, house-cleaning etc. My father was unable to get money through, but we did receive the occasional censored letter through the Red Cross and vice versa.

How did the war years affect me personally? I was too young to remember the first few years, but I do recall the horrible school lunches which were provided free to children, even evacuees from the Channel Islands, during the school holidays. I was too young to appreciate how lucky I was compared to the children in Jersey.

I do remember sirens and black curtains on the windows. We survived, and one of my vivid memories was when we received word that we were returning to Jersey. My mother grabbed my sister and me on to her lap and laughed and cried and hugged us.

I remember arriving back to the stranger who was my father and people not understanding my broad Yorkshire accent. I recall being upset because I couldn't go to school with my sister until I was six. I remember receiving a toy and a new dress from the Red Cross and lining up at the store for my sweets ration of Smarties.

This article first appeared in the Jersey Evening Post Freedom! supplement published to mark the 50th anniversary of the Liberation of Jersey

It is reprinted by kind permission of the Jersey Evening Post.

Helen, mother Dorothy and Pat Vivian.
Photo reproduced by kind permission of the Jersey Evening Post

MEMORIES OF THE EVACUATION IN JUNE 1940 AND THE WAR YEARS SPENT IN ENGLAND
by Margaret H. Newman (neé Hocquard)

In June 1940 my family left Jersey to spend the war years in Oxford. My father Edward Hocquard and his brother were in business as Hocquard Bros and they had an electrical business wiring houses as well as a shop in Beresford Street selling electrical appliances. Although I remember the vague feeling of unease at the time, it was from a child's perspective that my memories were formed. Obviously I was not aware of the implications of seeing men patrolling Victoria Avenue and the Esplanade wearing LDV armbands or of my mother stocking up on sugar and matches. I imagine a lot of discussion went on but "not in front of the children".

My uncle had served in the First World War and my father at 39 was still about military age. They had both been born in London and felt that there was a risk in remaining in the island in the event of German occupation, despite having a Jersey name and parentage.

On Wednesday 19 June the decision to leave was taken. My mother was in tears. One of her cousins had already left with her two small children, as her husband who worked at the airport had been drafted into the RAF.

Thursday 20 June was our D-Day.

My father left home about 6.00 am and drove to the airport as he realised that the boats were crowded. The story goes that at some point on the way, he met a friend who had already been to the airport to take his wife and her father there and he gave my father four tickets – I think they were probably tickets to wait in the queue rather than actual flight tickets.

When Father returned we packed two suitcases and my uncle had a small attaché case. Leaving the breakfast dishes on the table and the house keys with my grandfather, we set off at about 8.00 am. I think my father's friend drove us.

We spent the whole day waiting for our turn. I don't remember having any food but I think we must have had some sandwiches and I do remember my father giving us some chocolate. We eventually got on a plane about 4.00 pm. It was a 14 seater and there were 14 adults. My sister aged two years and I had to sit on our parents' knees and I seem to remember another small child at the back of the plane.

At one point during the flight, the door to the cockpit was opened and as we were at the front, I saw a gun propped up behind the pilot's seat. Presumably this was our defence against the Luftwaffe!

We flew to Bristol and then went by train to Oxford where my other grandmother was living with my two aunts, one of whom was a schoolteacher from London who had been evacuated with her school in 1939. We were told we had been on the last passenger plane to leave Jersey. The plane that left after us took airport personnel and documents. I have no way of knowing if this was the case.

We did not arrive in Oxford until 11.00 pm and it was in the blackout. We had to wake my grandmother by throwing pebbles at the window as they refused to answer the door as they thought we might be Germans! We had been unable to let them know we were coming.

As we were refugees from the Channel Islands, my father was not required to join the Forces and his skills were more useful in a factory building Spitfire parts, as he had been trained as a draughtsman on leaving school.

During the war we did receive and send Red Cross messages to my grandfather in Jersey. I think they were restricted to 25 words and there was a limit on how often they could be sent. The most important contacts were through the Channel Island Refugee Societies, which the Jersey Society in London was instrumental in setting up in various parts of the country. There was a branch in Oxford and my father was chairman. There were regular meetings on a Sunday afternoon in a church hall and mother had an allocation of tea, milk and sugar to provide a cup of tea for the members. News was exchanged and talks given. A Christmas party was held and the children were given a simple gift.

One talk in early 1945 was given by Roy Mourant and Peter Crill who had escaped from Jersey by boat. Roy's mother was a cousin of my father so we were able to get some family news.

Once a year there was a meeting in London for all the societies and my father and mother attended. It was an all day affair held in a large hall. These annual meetings were huge morale boosters as friends who lived in different parts of the country could be reunited and could provide information about others who had not been able to come.

On Christmas Day 1941 and 1942 the BBC broadcast a programme at lunchtime directed at the Channel Islands. The Islanders still had their radios and a miscellany of songs and readings was compiled to link up. My father, who had been active in musical circles and the Green Room Club in Jersey, sang and Daryl Quérée was also involved. The programme was pre-recorded in Bristol. We heard that many a tear was shed as songs like "Beautiful Jersey" and "The Dear Homeland" were sung. Once radios in the Islands had been confiscated the broadcasts were discontinued.

As I went to school in Oxford and grew up with my family, I do not think I had too many problems. I was in a place where there were many refugees from Europe – the children of Jewish academics who had been sent to friends and colleagues at the university. Their troubles were far greater and the Guernsey schoolchildren who were parted from their families had very different experiences. We did not see them as they had been sent to the North of England but the effects of that separation must have been difficult for many.

We arrived in England with very little and were very dependent on the kindness of our church friends who provided us with winter clothing, books and toys. In 1945 the family stayed in England. My sister and I were settled in school, my father had a good job and no business to go back to in Jersey and no capital to start again from scratch, so the decision was made to stay. Our house in St Saviour was sold and we have only returned for holidays but I am still a Jersey woman at heart and treasure my memories of being a little girl growing up in the Jersey of the 1930s.

THE MEMORIES OF BETTY LE BAIL née COLLAS

I was seven years old on 15 June 1940 and a couple of days later my family left Jersey – some of my birthday cake was left behind in a cupboard.

My parents (William and Elsie Collas) and my younger sister and brother were accompanied by Mum's parents and her sister. We travelled on a Dutch coal boat and as we neared the English coast the following morning one of the Dutch crewmen appeared with enamel pails full of hot tea and coffee. "Dip in, pigs" he called out in broken English! My parents and grandparents were not amused but excused him as he was a foreigner!

We stayed with friends of my family in Poole for three months, then moved to Surrey. We moved house five times and school four times, my father doing gardening jobs as they all provided living accommodation. Our final two years were spent in Godalming High Street as my father was "called up" to do factory work.

It was a typical early morning with children getting dressed for school and Mother urging haste and calling us for breakfast. Suddenly Dad rushed upstairs to our flat waving an envelope. There was great excitement as it was news from home – a "Red Cross" message! Everything else was forgotten for a few moments as we all stopped to hear the news, which was brief and more like a telegram than a letter.

Dad began reading …. "Young Charlie died as a result of accident." We were all stunned – excitement turned to shock and disbelief. "It can't be true. Read it again – read it again". But it was there, plain to see. "Young Charlie died as a result of accident." There were no other details, no explanation was possible. My mother cried, we children cried and poor Dad did his best to comfort us all.

Charlie was my big cousin and in Jersey he had lived with us with his widowed father and younger brother. This terrible news and the way we learned of it made the separation from our home and family even harder to bear. We felt so helpless – why did there have to be a war? Perhaps if we had stayed in Jersey we could have prevented such a terrible thing happening.

Much later we learnt that Charlie had been playing football in Millbrook Park when the ball rolled under a swing. He went to retrieve it but mistimed the movement and was struck by the swing in his abdomen. Charlie developed peritonitis and as the medical supplies and treatment available were so limited, he died aged just eighteen, on 8 June 1943.

The following was published by The Evening Post in June 1943.

THE PARK FATALITY
Inquest on Young Man killed by Swing

"Accidental death" was the verdict returned at the inquest held last Saturday afternoon at the General Hospital, before the Viscount, C.B.Le Gros Esq., and a jury, in the presence of C.S.Harrison Esq., Solicitor-General, and a jury on the body of Charles John Collas, the son of Mr Chas. Collas of "Altona", Kensington Place, who was fatally injured when he was struck in the stomach by a swing whilst playing in Coronation Park, Millbrook, the previous evening.

Mr A.C. Halliwell said Dr Darling rang him up on Friday morning to say that an accident case had been admitted. Witness called at the Hospital about 9.30 and saw the patient, who said he had been struck across the front of the stomach by an iron swing; he was conscious, but considerably shocked and clearly had received a serious internal injury. An operation was performed immediately; witness found deceased had a tear in the bowel called the "duodenum"; the cavity was full of fluid and there was peritonitis present. He sewed up the bowel but had very little hope that the patient would recover, because damage to that particular part of the bowel was usually fatal. Young Collas died the same day, death being due to a ruptured bowel and peritonitis. Any other part of the bowel could be sewn up and the patient usually recovered, but in a case like this one, the injury was such that the patient rarely recovered.

Centenier A.E.A. Tostevin of St Helier, said that on Friday morning he was informed from the Police Station that a young man named Collas had met with an accident at Coronation Park, Millbrook, and had been admitted to Hospital. In the morning he was informed that the lad had died. The Bailiff was notified and Centenier E.G.Pipon of St Lawrence made the necessary investigations.

Centenier E.G.Pipon of St. Lawrence said that on Friday about 12.30 he received a phone message from the Police Station informing him that a serious accident had occurred the previous evening in Coronation Park, Millbrook, a young lad named Charles John Collas having been seriously injured and admitted to the General Hospital. Witness was also requested to make enquiries about the accident. He ascertained that young Collas went to play a game of football in the park with a friend named Faiers and that, in running for the ball, he got near the swings on which there were two young fellows, and was struck in the stomach by the heavy swing. With the help of young Faiers, deceased managed to walk as far as Mrs. Faiers' residence, "Hughlea", Bel Royal, where he remained that night as he did not wish to be transferred to the Hospital. Next morning, Mrs. Faiers, seeing the lad in great pain, telephoned for the father as well as for Dr. Mortimer Evans. The latter ordered his immediate removal to the Hospital. Witness had also ascertained that the two lades on the swing were named Mortimer Francis Luce and Stephen Eugene Rousseau; they were about to get off the swing when the accident happened. According to the deceased's identity card, his name was Charles John Collas, born 6 May 1925 in St Helier.

Mr Charles John Collas, father of the deceased bore out the details given regarding name and date of birth. His son had been in the habit of going out to Bel Royal on Thursday and of staying there overnight. He was in good health when he left home just before mid-day on Thursday. Witness was informed of the accident the evening it happened, but was told that Dr. Sexton, who was actually attending young Faiers and who saw his son, said that there was nothing to worry about. Next morning he was called to proceed to Bel Royal and Dr Mortimer Evans, who was also called, also stated that there was nothing to worry about. Deceased told him that he was about to pick up the ball when the swing caught him.

Sydney Arthur Faiers and Mrs Faiers, his mother, were then called. The first named said deceased called to see them on Thursday morning as usual at "Hughlea", Bel Royal. In the afternoon they played football together in the park; the accident happened later in the evening; they decided to have a game of football together with other boy friends and the ball was shot past the "high flyer" – the biggest swing in the park. It seemed to swerve and strike deceased in the stomach; he was thrown about ten feet away, striking his head on a stone. The boys got off the swing and asked deceased if he was hurt; he said he would go and have a lie down in the shelter. They proceeded home later as deceased appeared to be in a "very bad way".

The game had only been in progress for a few minutes when the accident happened.

Mrs. Faiers corroborated her son's evidence. She asked Dr Sexton, who was at the house attending to her own son, to examine the deceased. She felt his pulse and said it was so good she did not think there was any serious injury; she wanted to give him an injection against shock, but he declined. She left some tablets to induce sleep and called back an hour and a half later; she again felt his pulse which was still good. She told witness that if he felt worse to telephone the Hospital. At midnight deceased was in such terrible pain that witness again phoned Dr Sexton who told her to give him a luminal tablet which induced sleep for about two hours. When deceased woke he was again in great pain, so she telephoned Dr Evans who came and examined the lad; he told the father there was nothing serious and nothing to worry about. Deceased, on the Doctor's recommendation, was later taken to the Hospital for observation.

Dr Mortimer, Frs. Luce and Stephen Eugene Rousseau corroborated the evidence regarding what took place in the park.

This concluded in evidence and, as stated, the jury returned a verdict of Accidental Death.

At this time, late 1943 early 1944, we were living on the first floor of a small factory in Godalming High Street. This was the fifth and final address in England. Both my parents worked in the factory which repaired servicemen's clothing.

The morning began like any other. It was just before the 8.00 a.m. BBC news and we were getting dressed for school. Dad was already downstairs to begin his work when suddenly the air raid siren began wailing. We were all rather surprised as we hadn't had a raid for some time, but almost immediately we were aware of the ominous drone of a plane. We recognized the engine sound of a V1 'doodlebug' coming nearer and nearer – louder and louder – and just when it seemed to be over the house the engine stopped. Mother was shouting "Under the beds. Get away from the windows" and we children were crying and very frightened. I seemed to freeze where I was on the landing, trying to avoid glass and forgetting a skylight above me. I burrowed among some coats on the hall stand and waited for the inevitable explosion. The house shook and so did I, but luckily the doodlebug came down a few hundred yards away. No-one was killed, but a house was sliced in half, and the windows of shops opposite us were blown out and people in a bus queue were cut by flying glass.

As soon as the noise of the explosion died down, we were aware of the dying wail of the siren and realised that the whole episode had taken less than the couple of minutes it took for the siren to sound its warning tone. Some warning! A few minutes later we heard the "All Clear".

D-Day came and went, and we were so upset when the Channel Islands were not liberated. We were more worried than ever for our families when Jersey was cut off from France – how would supplies get through? It seemed to us that Jersey had been forgotten and us too. We listened avidly to the BBC for news and the fate of the Islands seemed in the balance.

Eventually VE Day arrived and Mr Churchill actually referred to "Our dear Channel Islands" and we were "over the moon" with excitement. Street parties were organized in Godalming, but as we were the only children living in High Street, we didn't have one. Never mind, we were soon going home. We could now write letters home and my mother had a photograph taken of my brother and sister and myself to send home to show the family how we had all grown during the war.

What excitement!

Saying goodbye to school friends and neighbours was sad. We had been together for two years – a long time in a child's life. Promises of letters and future holidays in Jersey helped to soften the sad partings. We had to say a temporary "goodbye" to our grandparents who would be travelling home at a later date, but we returned to Jersey on 8 July 1945. Our grandparents returned three months later.

My father ran a small grocery shop in Kensington Place before the war, and as the States of Jersey wanted to encourage trade and business to get going again, we were given priority as soon as possible for an early passage home.

The train from Guildford to the south coast took us through terrible bomb damaged areas around London and the coastal regions, but eventually we set sail on a calm sea with a mine-sweeper clearing a safe passage for us.

As we neared the Jersey coast, the passengers became more and more excited pointing out familiar landmarks and singing "Beautiful Jersey". As we approached the pier heads, we could not believe our eyes. Everywhere along the entire pier and walks was crowded with people waving and calling out to their loved ones not seen for five long years. For a few brief moments we felt like Royalty stepping ashore.

My Uncle Jim arrived with his small truck to pick us up and at last we were home.   Everything was so strange – dreamlike at first – not really surprising after our five long years away. All our clothes and toys had gone – sold or given away to people who needed them during the Occupation. My dad's shop was bare save for a few small paper bags of flour, sugar, salt etc. Food was still in very short supply and we even received Red Cross parcels during our first few weeks home.

After a quick tour of our house, we rushed next door to see our aunt, uncles and cousins, and were relieved to find them reasonably healthy, if somewhat thinner than before the war. My paternal grandfather had died during the Occupation but my saddest home coming memory is of my Uncle Charlie (my father's brother) standing apart from all the joyous hugging and kissing, happy to see us all again but quietly weeping remembering his beloved son Charlie who should have been there sharing our joy, but had died in that accident in 1943.

Charles Collas

EVACUATION - THE MEMORIES OF MARGARET LANE

From Sunday 3 September 1939, England and Germany were at war. Paris surrendered to the Germans on 14 June 1940. In Jersey arrangements were made for a voluntary evacuation. The British Government sent ships to all the Channel Islands for people who wanted to leave.

It was rumoured that only women and children would be allowed to go but my parents decided to go only if my father could go too.

We were only allowed one suitcase each. There were six of us, Mum, Dad, Ken, John, Betty and myself. Ken was about 17 years old, I was 12, John was nine and Betty six. Mum packed what was necessary. Betty's teddy bear and doll were left on the stairs as she couldn't carry them. The front door was locked behind us and off we went walking to the harbour, which was packed with people waiting to board. Mum pushed Dad on first, for if he didn't get on, we wouldn't either.

Eventually we got on board this filthy ship, which was usually used to carry coal. We found a place to sit on deck for there were no passenger cabins on this boat! After a long wait we set off with no idea where we were going. It was jolly cold, I remember, and we had no food or water. Eventually one of the sailors brought us blankets and cups of tea.

Ken went to have a look around, found a mate of his and spent the journey in a life boat. He was filthy with coal dust when he came back to us.

I can't remember how long it took, but we eventually arrived in Weymouth and were taken to a large building where we were fed and watered. I don't know how long we were there before being put on a train for goodness knows where! What a horrible journey.

143

THE MEMORIES OF NORMAN LOUGHLIN

We were all staying at St Brelade's when my father drove out from town and told us that he had arranged for us to be on the boat for England the next day, as it was now certain that the Island was to surrender to the Germans. We were in the garden of the fisherman's cottage just above the harbour which we rented each year. Sadly during the Occupation it was blown up by the Germans but the remains of it are still there.

Those members of the family that left were my grandmother Mrs Maude du Feu and her daughters Mollie, Vera and Adele. Mrs Rita Loughlin (née du Feu) with her three children Richard aged 12, Norma, seven, and myself, Norman, aged four.

Initially my father Robin (Dick) Loughlin remained behind. He was the Head Steward of the United Club and had not made up his mind whether to follow us or stay and look after the Club. Eventually he was persuaded by a member of the Club Committee to join us and managed to get on the last boat. We were all very pleased to see him.

I remember our sea journey to England because we sat on a wooden bench on deck the whole way. My brother and sister ran around the deck as this was the first time that they had left Jersey and were treating it as a real adventure.

Mrs du Feu's other daughter, my aunt, was married and lived with her husband and daughter in Kingsbridge, South Devon.

It was at Kingsbridge that we all duly arrived. My mother and my grandmother sorted out where we were going to stay. For the time being my mother and my brother and sister and I stayed with my aunt and accommodation had been arranged with neighbours to take my grandmother and her daughters.

According to Winston Churchill, the war was going to last several years. That year, 1940, was a good summer and Kingsbridge would have been a perfect place if it hadn't been for the war. My father went to join up but was not accepted and, to this day, we never knew why. He eventually went to work for the BBC at their radio station at Start Point, where he remained until we left England. Mollie found work in a shop in Plymouth but was lucky to escape alive, as she was there the night of the Plymouth blitz. A little time after she joined the A.T.S. and served with them until the end of the war. Vera had worked at Gallichan the Jewellers and went to work for her brother-in-law at Boots the Chemist in Kingsbridge. Adale who had been deaf since about the age of 12 and could only speak and lip read Jersey French, helped out in my aunt's house as there was a lot of extra work in keeping the place clean.

My father and mother managed to find spacious accommodation above a grocer's at the foot of Fore Street in Kingsbridge where we stayed until 1945.

It was here that we all experienced probably the worst day of the war. On a Saturday lunchtime in June 1943 the Germans had flown up the estuary from Salcombe and dropped several bombs on Kingsbridge. I was six years old and, for many years could remember the deafening noise and smell. All our windows blew in, all the ceilings came down and all the soot came down the chimney. It soon became clear that we had been very lucky as the whole street was on fire and in ruins and we were the only building still standing.

On the night of the blitz on Plymouth, my father became worried about the amount of planes flying over us and decided that we should go up into the fields above Kingsbridge. He wrapped me in an eiderdown and we stayed looking across towards Plymouth. The whole sky was lit up with the continual bombing which we could hear as dull thuds. Finally in the early morning it all went quiet but the sky remained red.

On another visit by the Germans they targeted the grammar school but it was after school time and most of the boys, including my brother, were out but a master and some boys were still in the school and died in the raid.

One of the houses where the Loughlin family lived until it was bombed

The Loughlin family. Left to right, Vera du Feu, her mother Maude Du Feu Norma and Richard Loughlin, Robin (Dick) and Rita Loughlin, Adele du Feu and on the lawn, Mollie du Feu and Norman Loughlin.
The window is covered in paper strips in case of bomb blast.

THE MEMORIES OF LT COMMANDER JOHN MAIN WADDELL

Jersey Airways operated flights between the Channel Islands and the United Kingdom from 1933, initially bringing holidaymakers and then business people to the Islands. However, before too long Islanders began to use the services regularly even though Jersey's airport at the time was West Park beach and the terminal a motor coach which could be driven off the beach at high tide.

The States Airport opened in 1937 and Jersey Airways' fleet expanded to include larger aircraft and early morning services were introduced bringing both mail and national newspapers. In addition, if there was a need for urgent or special medical attention, the authorities would call on their 'flying ambulance' service to take patients to the mainland.

During this time, John Main Waddell was one of the pilots employed by Jersey Airways.

With the outbreak of war, the airline operated under a special arrangement with H.M. Government and in addition to their general services other duties were frequently undertaken by their pilots and aircraft.

Once it became apparent that the enemy advance through France might lead to the occupation of the Channel Islands, the services of the airline were withdrawn from the Islands and all operations were transferred to mainland Britain. It was thought that this would take a week, in fact it was actually carried out in two days.

As the transfer was taking place, the wives and families of the Jersey Airways' staff were flown to England where they were found accommodation and as thoughts turned to friends in Jersey it was decided to try and get them out of the Island..

Permission to operate flights from an airport in the west of England was granted and available aircraft were transferred to that base. It was considered desirable that the aircraft should operate with volunteer crews. Without exception all the flying personnel responded, eager to help although the position regarding the demilitarisation of the Channel Islands was explained to them.

The very first evacuation service left England at 5.00 a.m. on 19 June 1940 and flew on a course which had previously been laid down by the

147

aviation authorities. A volunteer ground staff had remained in Jersey, along with traffic staff to attend to reservations and loading the aircraft. The usual formalities were dispensed with to save time, and tickets were issued only on arrival in England.

Single fares were charged, although their collection was in some cases conveniently forgotten as there were Islanders whose circumstances were such that the company felt justified in turning a blind eye. Long queues started to collect outside the Airport buildings and as an aircraft landed the people to fill it were taken off the front of the queue.

In all about four hundred passengers left the Island, with Jersey Airways finishing their sterling work by 21 June.

Among the four hundred people were sunbathers direct from the beach, farmers from their fields and mothers and children looking for their husbands. Most of them were taking their very first journey by air and fortunately the weather conditions were ideal.

On arrival in England Jersey Airways staff did all they could to help. Railway schedules were arranged, relatives and friends telegraphed with news of arrivals. Many travelled to London's Waterloo Station where staff from the Jersey Airways London office were there to help and assist, while the Women's Voluntary Service gave as much help as they could.

On a lighter note, one old lady was asked on arrival by Customs officers if she had anything to declare. From a large pocket in her skirt, she immediately pulled a revolver explaining that she had intended to use it to defend herself against German parachutists! Unfortunately, all this was said in Jersey French, causing great confusion and concern until an interpreter could be found.

John Main Waddell went on to a distinguished career in the Fleet Air Arm. By 1941 he was the Commanding Officer in charge of Squadron 783 on HMS Condor at Arbroath and in December of that year he was appointed as Senior Air Officer on HMS Victorious with responsibility for advising Admiral Sir John Tovey, first in Scapa Flow and later when Victorious was sent to the Mediterranean to cover the North African landings.

From then until May 1945 he was Commanding Officer of HMS Grebe in Alexandria.

In 1945 John Waddell received a letter from Mr G.O. Walters, general manager of Jersey Airways. It read:

8th August 1945

Dear Waddell,

I have pleasure in enclosing herewith a letter from the Air Ministry in which they inform is that the Company's claim on your behalf for the award of the 1939/45 Star has been approved.

In forwarding this I would like to express the appreciation of the Directors and Management that your efforts in connection with the "Evacuation Services" have been official recognized.

Yours sincerely,

G.O.Walters

Sadly John Main Waddell died in 1947 as a result of the war and is commemorated on a Commonwealth War Graves monument in South London Crematorium, Mitcham. His papers are now in Fleet Air Arm Museum at Yeovilton in Devon.

From paperwork held by his son, Gavin Main Waddell, and reproduced with his permission.

THE MEMORIES OF JIM RICHARDS

Our father had already left the Island and was serving in the British Army, and we spent our last evening in Jersey at the Great Western Hotel, owned by my godfather Alf Blake, it having been agreed that it would be best if we left the Island. We left on what we believed was one of the last mailboats.

Having arrived safely in England, we went north to Barnsley to stay with my aunt Grace Smith. After spending some time there, for some reason or other we had to leave with nowhere to go. As young as I was I can remember the three of us, my mother May, my brother Derek and me, standing under a gas street lamp crying our eyes out. It was cold, dark and misty when a guardian angel in the form of an Irish lady by the name of Mrs Redman asked why we were crying. Our mother told her we had nowhere to go. Mrs Redman took us in. I am not sure how long we stayed with the Redman family (they had two daughters) but our mother kept in touch with them for many years and in fact they visited us in Jersey. The last time we saw the daughters was in 1981 when my mother, Derek, myself and my wife were on holiday in Llandudno in north Wales.

From Barnsley we had to go south to Bournemouth because of Derek's ill health. On the way we had to stay overnight in London and because of the air raids we spent the night on the platform of an Underground station along with many others. A Pearly King and Queen kept us entertained singing all the old songs of the time with everyone joining in.

When we finally arrived in Bournemouth we went to stay with an elderly gentleman, Mr Harding, who was an A.R.P. warden. He lived at 113 Norcroft Road, with our mother acting as his housekeeper in return for us living there. I remember Mr Harding for his big moustache, his butterfly/moth collection and the smell of Marmite and Bovril.

For most of the war our father was a prisoner of war, being among those captured at Dunkirk. The three of us used to attend the Channel Islands Association meetings where sometimes our mother used to get up on the stage dressed in a blue and white gingham dress and recite a little something or other. Once or twice she tried to raffle us off but luckily for us there were no takers!

One day just as our mother was about to leave the house to go shopping a police car pulled up with our father inside. They came down the road to the school I was attending to fetch me home. It was strange at first but I soon got used to him. It took Derek a little longer being a bit on the shy side.

In the June or July of 1945 we left Southampton on the midnight mailboat (we spent the journey sitting outside on life rafts) to return to Jersey. We lived in Grève d'Azette for a number of years and I attended St Luke's School. Ray and May passed away some years ago. Derek still lives on the Island in St Martin while I live in Birmingham.

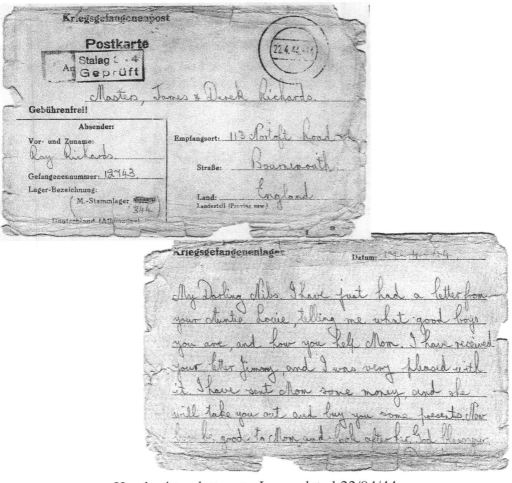

Handwritten letters to James dated 22/04/44

ERNIE LE BRUN'S STORY PRESENTED BY HIS WIDOW ANNE

In June 1940 Mr Ernest Le Brun took his wife Evelyn and their six children down to the Albert Pier to be evacuated to England. He then returned to Sorel Farm to attend to the cattle hoping to join them on the boat. Unfortunately, as with many others, he was left behind as there was no more room on the boat and nor were there any others.

Mrs Le Brun and the children were sent to Bolton and in July 1943 they had their photograph taken. They then asked a Mrs P Jarrett if she would send it to Mr Vernon Jarrett, who was in a camp in Germany. Vernon Jarrett then sent it to his mother, Mrs H Jarrett of Central Stores, St John, who passed it on to Mr Ernest Le Brun so that he knew that his family were safe.

Mrs Le Brun and her children arrived back in Jersey on one of the first boats in June 1945.

Ernest Le Brun's family

152

THE NOEL FAMILY DURING 1940 TO 1945
JANET I. FERBRACHE (née NOEL) REMEMBERS

It is said that a two and a half year old child cannot remember details of that time in their past but I have described events to my mother which she did not recall but were later proved to be correct.

My parents Clarence (Clarry) George and Adele Noel, née Le Marquand, were saying a sad farewell at the harbour (as Dad felt unable to leave his work) when a friend said, "Clarry, you are not going to cope when the Germans come – why don't you 'hop' on to the boat and join your family?" Dad gave him the keys to our car and – with no luggage – did just that. Dad had had his whole left leg amputated when, at only 23 years of age, he had sarcoma cancer.

On board ss Archangel he was warmly welcomed by my Mum, my five year old brother Robert and myself – Janet. We travelled with our relations, John and Dorothy Le Marquand and their son David, Ralph and Elsie Le Marquand with their twins, Margaret and Mary and son Brian, and Mum's friend Madeleine (Maddy) Hibbs.

On arrival in Southampton we all stayed the night at a friend's home before travelling by train to Liverpool where we separated from our relations. Another friend, Flora Cann, drove us to her isolated bungalow near Mold in North Wales, where we stayed on our own for three weeks.

As Dad could not find work, we took up a kind offer to stay with friends, Bert and Joyce Rumble in Coventry, where Dad and Maddy started work at No.1 factory, Standard Motor Company (Aero-engines) at Fletchamstead – in the plating department.

Little did we realise what a dangerous area we had settled in as very soon the bombing started and the 'Blitz' caused much loss of life day and night. It was so traumatic that I have never forgotten the noise and being carried nightly down to the garden air raid shelter by my Mum – as Dad obviously could not help.

After a heavy raid a man called on my Dad to ask him his shoe size as a shoe shop had been bombed and two size eight men's right lace up shoes were all that had been left from the window display – these fitted and Dad wore them for the duration of the war!

Three months later my Mum took Robert and me to live in Denbigh, North Wales, to escape the bombing. Dad stayed in Coventry as he needed the work. Mum, Robert and I were joined in Denbigh by Mum's brother Ralph and his family and later by her cousin Cyril and his wife May and their daughters, Elaine and Denise. This was great as Robert and I grew up with uncles, aunts and cousins which helped overcome the sadness of being parted from our Jersey folk.

My Dad left his factory job as he developed dermatitis caused by cadmium fumes and this kept recurring. The enforced reason for leaving Coventry was a blessing to Dad as he had faced many dangerous situations. The worst time was when he got off the train one night at the wrong station – as the place names had all been covered up. He had to find his way in pitch darkness over the rubble of damaged houses and walking with only one leg and using crutches he was terrified of falling. It took him two hours to find his lodgings and the folk he was staying with were very worried. That night between 7 p.m. and 6 a.m. twenty two bombs dropped in the field opposite and blew out all their windows and damaged the roof while they huddled in the air raid shelter.

Although living safely in Denbigh, Dad found getting work very difficult as there were many other men disabled by the war who were similarly seeking employment. He supervised two hundred Liverpool evacuees before being employed by the council office as Billeting Officer. Mum made and sold smocked dresses for babies and did hairdressing.

Robert and I were educated without charge at a small private school as the headmistress said this was her 'war effort'. At 10 years old Robert won a scholarship to the Grammar School which was later' 'honoured' at Victoria College when we returned home.

We moved three times before being offered a 'two up, two down' cottage with no bathroom and a shared outside toilet – this was our first time not sharing a house which was great!

As Dad had played the organ in churches in Jersey he was asked to play at the Vale Street church where, each week, Robert and I were expected to recite a verse from the Bible and at seven years old I sang solos. The Guernsey Ladies College had evacuated to Denbigh and the girls were also involved in our lives through the church.

Although we only had two small bedrooms we somehow had many evacuee relations and friends to stay with us.

Because Mum had to cut off one leg of Dad's new flannel trousers the spare material was used to make clothes for me – how I wished he would buy some pink or blue ones instead of grey or brown!!

I well remember VE day when everyone was dancing in our lane and having a street party. We were lucky to be able to return to Jersey quite soon as Dad was asked to help at Le Marquand's Garage, Bel Royal, as the owner, Mum's cousin Philip, was a Royal Navy Commander and could not return to Jersey for some time.,

We had a shock when we saw the state of our house as the Germans had occupied it for the five years, so we lived with my grandfather, Jurat John Le Marquand, and my Aunt Ida until we could move back to our own home.

My parents certainly coped well and overcame many problems during the war but we had many happy times and as I get older I realise how much I have to thank them for.

Janet with her parents
and brother Robert

155

THE MEMORIES OF NANCY LE CLERCQ née TROY

I was 13 when we were evacuated to England. I travelled with my mother and three little brothers, Tony (four), Colin (two and a half) and Brian (ten months) while my two other brothers, Edward (15) and John (8), were sent to Eccles with their school. Dad stayed behind to sort out his building firm and followed as a few days later, arriving on the last boat to leave the Islands. On the day he left the docks were bombed and he had to shelter before boarding the ship. Several people were killed.

When we arrived at Weymouth we were taken to a large hall and stayed there for several days sleeping on camp beds laid out in rows. Each day people came to offer to take some of the children to care for until the war was ended but my Mum, bless her, never let anyone take us: she was determined that we would all stay together.

On our first day in Weymouth sirens sounded and we had to make our way to a shelter. Mum carried Brian, I carried Colin and poor little Tony had to walk. He was so frightened that he lay down in the road and started to cry. Luckily a policeman came along, lifted Tony up, put him on his shoulders and took us all to the shelter. We couldn't thank him enough for his kindness.

After a few days we were put on a train and told we were being sent up North. We travelled all night but had no idea where we were as all the station nemaes were blacked out. We ended up in Lancashire and settled in Bury. We stayed in a municipal hall for about a week until we were allocated a house. Firstly we stayed in a two-bedroomed house in Goldfisher Drive and Mum set about getting my brothers Edward and John back to live with us. After Dad arrived we moved a couple of doors down the road to a three-bedroomed house, 112 Ferngrove, where we settled down to a very different lind of life that the somewhat sheltered existence we had been used to in Jersey; different ways, people, food, accents, smoke and even wool floating in the air from the factories. This was wartime Britain. But I remember most of all the kindness and helpfulness of the people we met and we made many friends.

Dad managed to get a job as a carpenter and Mum made a home for us out of a few sticks of furniture we had kindly been given and any bits and pieces we could find. We only had the few clothes we had been anble to bvring with us and although we were allocated clothing coupons, most of them had to be used for my little brothers because they were growing all the time. We learned to make do and mend and became very inventive. When we went out we put gravy browning on our legs and drew a line down the back to make it look like we were wearing stockings. What a mess! We stood in line whenever we saw a queue without knowing what was on offer. Sometimes it was only an orange.

I had to go to school for a term because my birthday was on 17 September, a few days after the school term started. That winter we found it very cold as we only had summer clothes. A lady teacher took pity on us and told Olive, another girl from Jersey, and me that we could stay inside at playtime because we were not used to the cold weather. Then along came our class teacher, a man, who sent us to the Headmaster for staying in! We were both caned on our hands and thought it was so unfair since the other teacher had told us we could stay inside. We were often asked to read in front of the class as the teacher said we pronounced words 'properly'. We didn't pick up the Northern accent (as some of the younger children did) because we were that much older.

I left school in December 1940 when I was 14 and went to work in Bensons Toffee Factory. We were allowed to eat as many sweets as we liked during working hours but were not allowed to take any home. However we always managed to find ways of sneaking a few out for the boys and luckily we were never caught. I didn't work there for very long as they had difficulty getting sugar and other ingredients ande went to work in a shoe factory. I worked from 8.00 am until 6.00 pm and some days until 8.00 pm – no easy working hours then.

In winter it was very cold with snow and ice. Our short cut to work was down a bumpy lane through a field and in places I had to crawl because it was so slippery. I bought a pair of trousers to wear to save my legs. Dad was horrified when he saw me wearing then for the first time. In those days women never wore trousers; it was just not done. I can still see poor Mum, usually so elegantly dressed, coming up the road with socks over her shoes to stop her slipping on the icy pavements, pushing a pram loaded with bags of coal. My brothers used to make sledges out of anything they could find, the backs of old chairs, wooden boxes and old trays.

They had great fun sliding down slopes – we had never seen so much snow.

On Saturday afternoons my friend Evelyn Conroy and I would go to the park to watch the boys play football. They used to call us their mascots because at half time we used to give them an orange (if we could get one) or some water.

At Christmas Dad, Mum and I usede to make toys for my brothers. One year Dad made blackboards and Mum and I knitted golliwogs. Unfortunately we were unable to finish the last one in time so we decided to leave a note for Father Christmas telling my brother Tony to ask either Mum or me to help finish it. Luckily for us Tony was more thrilled to receive a letter from Father Christmas that to have his golliwog. Sadly we never did get round to finishing it and I felt so sorry what when we returned to Jersey at the end of the war I made him another one. Of course he was much too old for a knitted toy by then and we all laughed about it.

Dad was chairman of the Bury and District Channel Islands Society for most of the war years and he was presented with a brass carriage clock inscribed with his name and the length of time he served, with many thanks from the Jersey people. My brother John has the clock now and it is still in working order. At the meetings we sometimes had concerts and singalongs and Dad used to get me up on stage to sing. In 1944 Dad went down to London to work as a welfare officer assisting people who had been bombed out. He remained there until the war ended and we were able to return to Jersey again.

Looking back, I think my parents made a very brave decision for us to evacuate as their lives were turned upside down. With the Germans approaching they left their home and families behind to an unknown fate to go to who knew where, with little money, no possessions and only the clothes they stood up in because they first thought was to get their children away to safety. Who could blame them for that?

THE EVACUATION OF JUDY LE LIEVRE née Carter

The night before we left Jersey, on 24 June 1940, I went with my mother to the Town Hall to get the tickets; my father had died the year before.

The ship was called Archangel and was an old cargo boat. At first only women and children were being accepted, so my older brothers came down to the boat to see us off. Of course, my mother was crying and a policeman said, "Why don't you all go – there's plenty of room".

So they all came with us although they had no luggage – only the clothes they were wearing. All we had was a few things in pillowcases as we did not have any suitcases.

On the boat we met our aunt who was there with her children. She was given a cabin because she was very seasick and she had a baby only five weeks old with her.

My mother went to help her with the baby and it was a very long tiring journey.

When we arrived in Southampton there was a train waiting for us all.I was only ten and I remember the big train and thought it was very exciting.

We spent hours on the train and I do remember that someone gave us bars of chocolate and sandwiches. When we arrived in the north of England, they split the train in two – one half went to Barnsley and the other went to Bury.

We went to Barnsley and the people there were very pleased to hear us speaking English. They had thought we were going to be Belgium evacuees!

For the first few days in Barnsley we lived in a big church hall and slept on the floor. A couple of days later we had tables and chairs for us to eat our meals. The people in charge wanted us to go to billets with Yorkshire families, but my mother did not want us to be separated and in the end about six families were housed in an old rectory and the generous Yorkshire people donated clothes and furniture for all of us.

Two of my older brothers had already enlisted in the Royal Air Force and after a few days they went to an RAF camp. Not long after this, another brother, Jim, claimed he was seventeen (although he was only sixteen) and he also joined the RAF.

That left two boys, my mother and myself. My oldest brother, George, was married with two small children and he managed to rent a house for all of us to be together. My aunt and her family lived just around the corner.

George went to work in Sheffield in an aircraft factory, but he was not happy there and he too joined the RAF. As the two brothers with us grew up they also joined up, this time in the Navy, leaving my mother and me, my sister in law and her children, together with her mother and sister who had also left Jersey and who joined us in the house.

My five years in Barnsley were very happy ones; I was at school for four years and worked in a shop during the last year.

I will always love the Yorkshire people. They were the kindest and most generous people I have ever met.

At first only women and children were being accepted for evacuation

EVACUATION --- THE LE COCQ FAMILY STORY
by Maurice Le Cocq

When the announcement was made that all people born in England should evacuate the Island, my mother immediately decided that the family should go, although she had very divided loyalties. Even though she was of a good Jersey family, the Le Bretons, she had been born in England. Her father Adolphus had left the Island in 1896 with his wife and family in search of work. My mother was born the following year but returned to the Island when she was seven. However, she was worried that her place of birth would count against her, and she was also swayed by the fact that one of her children was seriously ill. She was torn in two as her parents had decided that they would stay in Jersey, but for the sake of the children, who they feared would not fare well under the German occupation, my parents decided to go.

This was a big undertaking for my mother as she had five children. She had only given birth five weeks previously to twins, one of whom had died at birth. The other was me.

The decision to go was made and having made her farewells to her parents she made her way to the quay with her children, carrying the youngest, myself, in her arms. My father decided that he needed to return the works van and the previous day's takings to his place of employment, Cooper & Company, the tea and coffee merchants in Halkett Place, and agreed to meet her down at the harbour. Somehow, and it was never exactly established how, the cargo boat Archangel sailed without him and my mother was left on her own to care for her children. The Captain took pity on her and gave her the use of his cabin for the duration of the journey because she was so unwell.

Once we arrived in Southampton the authorities sent our group of evacuees by train to Barnsley in Yorkshire. It was an exhausting journey both for my mother and the younger children, though exciting for the older ones.

We were lucky for we were given good accommodation, and soon settled in, but my mother and the older children worried about the whereabouts of my father. We were all afraid that he had been trapped in Jersey for the duration of the war, and it was a very worrying time. One of my older brothers, Derrick, who had been ill before he left Jersey, was found to have tuberculosis which had not been diagnosed in Jersey and was sent to hospital, where he spent two years. Soon after our arrival I too was ill, and was also sent to hospital where I spent the next 18 months recovering from diphtheria.

After we had been in Barnsley about three months there was a knock on the door and when my sister answered it she saw my father standing there resplendent in a Royal Air Force uniform. He had been searching for us, having caught the next boat out of Jersey. On landing he had enquired where the last boat load of evacuees had been sent and was told Scotland, so he travelled up there in search of us. Unfortunately our boat had landed in Southampton, his boat had landed in Weymouth, and so he had been sent after the wrong lot of evacuees. Having failed to find us he had decided to join up, though actually too old he had lied about his age, and nothing had been said as they were only too glad to have him as he was a mechanic by trade. He was posted to an airfield down south where he helped to keep the aircraft flying, so he was away for the whole of the war and my mother was left to cope as best as she could. Luckily her sister in law and her children had also been sent to Barnsley and they lived just around the corner from us so she had some familiar faces around her.

My oldest brother, Cyril, was just 16 but he decided to join the Navy and lied about his age. He was sent to serve on a minesweeper with the Arctic convoys, which was a dreadful experience for such a young man. My sister chose to do war work and got a job in a factory packing parachutes which she seemed to quite enjoy. She and her fellow workers would put notes in the parachutes of their names and addresses, and one day a young man arrived at the door asking for her. It turned out that his life had been saved by a parachute that she had packed, and he had made the journey to Yorkshire to say 'thank you', and to take her out. She was delighted.

I don't have any early memories of my time as an evacuee as I was too young, and I was in hospital for such a long time, but after I came out of hospital I remember going to school in Barnsley with my brother who was a couple of years older than me, and I have vague recollections of the air raid shelter. I also remember the mighty singsongs to drown the sound of the bombs falling.

One of my earliest recollections is of my father coming home on leave in his uniform. I had never seen him before, having been in hospital and I was terrified of men in uniform, so I ran and hid behind the settee. It took him quite a while to get me to come out and that was only with the help of a Mars Bar. The temptation was too great and I crept out and grabbed it. As he was home so rarely, I never really got used to the fact that he was my father until after the war.

My abiding memory of my time as an evacuee was the bonfire which we held on VE Day. Together with our neighbours we built a massive bonfire against the garden wall and there were huge celebrations. The fire was so big that more than 50 years later, when I returned to Yorkshire with my father and went to visit the house in Barnsley, the wall was still blackened and damaged where the fire had been.

Once my father and brother had been demobbed my mother was keen to get back to Jersey. We travelled down to London by train where we had to change trains and I can clearly remember that my mother insisted on feeding the dog, which we had acquired during the war, on Paddington station, much to the embarrassment of my sister. Peter the dog had not been left in Yorkshire but travelled back to Jersey with us.

On her arrival back in Jersey my mother was devastated to discover that her mother had not survived the Occupation. We had nowhere to live and had to move in with relatives until such time as we could find a house of our own to rent. After seeing what the Jersey people had been through my mother was glad that she had chosen to leave as she felt sure that both my brother Derrick and I would not have survived. She also felt that bad as rationing had been the family had fared better than the town people in Jersey who had been on starvation rations, while we always had enough to eat, albeit not what we might have chosen.

THE MEMORIES OF SUSAN HUMPLEBY

I was four months old when my parents and I evacuated from Jersey in June 1940. The reason we left was due to the fact that my father, having fought in the Great War, saw how women were treated by the Germans. We went to Bitterne, Southampton, where my father worked in the aircraft factory. One day he was at work when the Germans bombed the building, when not only was his body riddled with shrapnel, he almost lost the use of his right arm. He was taken to Sparkbrook Hospital which was where badly burned Royal Air Force men were taken.

While Southampton was being bombed, everyone ran for the shelters but in the flurry of activity Mum forgot all about me and it was only when someone asked where I was that she realised I was still in the house and she had to run back to get me. Naturally I do not know very much about this as I was only seven months old at the time.

After a short time in Reading , we moved to 24 Norham Road, Oxford, where we lived with a family by the name of Sturt. I believe my mother was like a housekeeper there, and she also did District Nursing as she had previously worked at the Dispensary (now the Le Bas Centre) in St Saviour's Road from 1930 to 1939. During the war my father worked for the BBC in London.

I began my schooldays at Greycoats and I still have one of their badges; it was around this time that it was discovered that I was deaf in both ears. According to what I have been told, we had to go to Manchester to find help for this.

The Sturt family were very nice people and the daughter Susan was told to look after me by taking me out boating, on walks and to the park which was not very far away. I was told that I used to bring back frogs from the park to put in the back garden. We even slept in a tent as well.

On one occasion the whole family had a break for a few days in Weston Super Mare. Again, according to what I was told, the landlady was not very nice and one day when she was out my mother persuaded my father to have a decent bath using all the hot water the landlady had saved up for herself. She was not very pleased when she found out !

I remember the surroundings where we lived, and one day one of the houses caught fire and I walked on the firemen's hoses which were lying on the pavement.

When, in 1944, the late Bailiff, Sir Peter Crill, escaped from Jersey and arrived in England, he came to visit my parents in Oxford with news of the Island.

Just after the war finished we went to a circus where I saw an elephant for the first time, and was taken to skate and go on the dodgem cars.

After the war, my father returned to the Island on his own, as his own father had died just before the Liberation. My mother and I came home in November 1945 where we stayed with relatives at Georgetown, before moving to Simon Place.

It was not until nearly four years later in December 1949, that I began wearing a hearing aid.

Crowds gather near the harbour before boarding the boats to England

THE MEMORIES OF BETTY GATES née BISSON

In June 1940 our grandfather from Scotland was in Jersey on holiday with his family. My mother was his daughter and with my stepfather, little sister Margaret and big brother Philip, we were a happy crowd, living together at La Pouquelaye.

Then came the news that the Germans were coming ! My grandfather begged my mother to take him back to Scotland as he remembered the Germans from the Great War.

So my parents went to the Town Hall to find thousands of people milling around, all bewildered and wondering what to do. There was a man standing on the steps called us "dirty rats" for leaving a sinking ship, but nevertheless mother was told to go to the harbour with one case per person, where we would find a boat. She came home, packed our little cases, closed the door leaving behind Fluffy the Persian cat. My poor mother sobbed her heart out.

When we arrived at the docks a boat had come in packed with soldiers from Dunkirk, but the captain said he would take as many as possible; we were lucky to get on board where we went to the galley and the sailors gave us 'dog biscuits' and tea. Then they locked us in ...

After 19 hours at sea we arrived at Southampton where we were sent to an ice rink until the next day after which we were sent to Wakefield.

At that time the authorities wanted to split up families to put them into lodging, but my stepfather was having none of that especially as my grandfather was so close to his home in Scotland.

It was decided that we would go on our way, and arrived in Scotland where the people were exceptionally kind; I already knew that because my mother herself was Scottish.

We lived in Renfrew on the Clyde and arrived in time to settle in for the winter air-raids. It really was the most horrendous time, living most nights in an Anderson shelter, or under the bed when the bombs were falling. While we were there, my 14 year old brother was sent to a local shipyard as an apprentice, while I went to Johnston Heights school, and my eight year old sister Margaret went to Thornhill Primary School. We children treated our time in Renfrew almost as a holiday as we met many of our relatives there whom we might never had met had we stayed in Jersey.

When I was 13 years old, my stepfather opened a shoe repair shop in Johnstone but, because he could not get any young men to work with him, he got me an exemption from school and taught me the trade. It was quite a novelty repairing shoes in a shop window and my greatest thrill was to see the troop of R.E.M.E. soldiers marching past everyday who all nodded and winked at me – by then a very impressionable 15 year old girl.

We came home in September 1945 when I celebrated my 18th birthday and we stayed in the Chelsea Hotel until my parents found somewhere to live. We did go back to see our rented house at La Pouquelaye, but of course by that time all our personal effects had been taken from it, so we actually came back to nothing.

At first I continued my 'trade' as a shoe repairer but did not keep it up as I thought I would never find a boyfriend while I reeked of leather! I worked at George D. Laurens and Orviss, while my brother Philip joined the forces, and Margaret went back to school.

It all sounds so ordinary now, but was traumatic at the time, and it was lovely to be home again in Jersey.

Betty with her brother and sister

THE MEMORIES OF EVE BATTRICK née BOURKE

I was born on 24 November 1935 in a rented house called "Crediton" opposite Samares Manor, St Clement. My mother, Lilian Florence Bourke (known as Nin), lived there with her parents Lysle Martin and Florence Evelyn Bourke and her brother Martin George Bourke (known as George). Nin was unmarried so, as often happened at that time, I was raised as her sister and called Evelyn Bourke.

George and his fiancée Margaret Fairhurst (known as Peggy) had planned their wedding in Jersey for July 1940 but they quickly rearranged it and were married at St Luke's Church on 20 June. We were unable to attend because we had to catch the boat. Incidentally I was due to be a bridesmaid at their wedding and one of my memories is seeing my lovely lavender coloured organza bridesmaid dress hanging in the bedroom. Sadly we left it behind. George and Peggy left Jersey by boat on 21 June. He wanted to use his skills to contribute to the war effort.

Dad managed to get permits for 20 June 1940 for Mum, Nin and I to leave the Island – women and children first was the order of the day which was why he did not travel with us.

I can remember it was a warm summer's day and we travelled on a very dirty coal boat and I was very sad because we also had to leave our dog behind. We gave the dog to a neighbour who had decided to stay in Jersey.

I believe the journey took longer that expected due to the suspected presence of U-boats in the English Channel and we arrived on the south coast where we all slept in a hall overnight. Unfortunately, we had very few possessions as we were only allowed to take one small suitcase each weighing not more that 25 lbs.

The next day we travelled north to Barnsley in Yorkshire by train which took a very long time as we stopped at various stations and were kindly greeted by members of the Salvation Army who gave us thick corned beef sandwiches and mugs of tea sweetened with condensed milk. The weather was hot and sunny and the children wanted water. Mum would not allow me to drink the train water – just as well because some who did later contracted diphtheria.

When we finally arrived we were all billeted in an Ebenezer Chapel, given our first hot meal for several days which consisted of very salty sausage and mash. That night we slept in our clothes on camp beds with white blankets. Because the children had drunk a lot of water most of us wet the bed and the adults who wore dark clothes were covered in white fluff from the blankets.

We did not know what happened to Dad, but after a week he found us – he was lucky as he left Jersey on the very last boat.. He was also keen to help the war effort. He had been a Quartermaster Sergeant in the Middlesex Regiment in the Great War but he was too old for this one. During the war older men took the place of the younger ones who served in the armed forces.

As George was a champion radio ham he immediately joined the Royal Signals, while Peggy went to stay with her mother and relations in Wellington, Shropshire. George was posted to work in the War Office in London and was there during the Blitz. He was then trained at Bletchley Park (famous for decoding Enigma), then in 1941 he was posted to serve with the British Military Mission in Moscow and travelled on one of the Russian convoys. He was there throughout the war during which time he was "Mentioned in Dispatches" for dedication to duty and also awarded the British Empire Medal.

On being demobbed in 1946 he went back to Bletchley Park for more training, then he was asked to join the Foreign Service because of his knowledge of Russia and his language skills and he took up a position of as member of the Diplomatic Radio Corps. He was posted to Bucharest in Rumania and remained there until May 1950. when he was finally granted leave. Apparently the reason for the delay was because of staff shortages and the fact that the Rumanian authorities were reluctant to issue a visa for his replacement. I believe too that there were also some serious spy trials taking place in Bucharest at the time.

He travelled back to London on a three day overland journey accompanied by the King's Messenger. Tragically George died on 8 May 1950, the very day he arrived in London and while still on active service. One month later Peggy died in Shropshire of tuberculosis and a broken heart. In ten years of marriage they had spent barely one year together due to the war and the subsequent Cold War. George had always promised her they would be together for their 10th Wedding Anniversary – they were "in death"

As they had no children I feel it is my duty to record their lives.

Back in Barnsley Dad, Mum, Nin and I were eventually allocated an empty house by the Council which we shared with some other people. Our kind hearted neighbours donated bits of furniture and household equipment to help us settle in. Dad found work as an insurance agent and Nin worked as a grocery assistant.

Mum had a heart condition and suffered badly from the first harsh winter so Dad managed to transfer with the same company to Guildford in Surrey. He later worked in the goods office of Southern Railway and Nin worked in Holden's Grocery Store. They both also worked as Air Raid Wardens and were constantly on duty.

In Guildford we shared a small bungalow with Mr and Mrs Mitchell and their daughter. This was situated near the Fire Station on the London to Portsmouth by-pass. There was a great shortage of houses and possessions during the war and everyone shared what they had and helped each other out.

I attended Stoke Park Primary School and made friends. Life settled into a good routine until we were bombed out by a doodlebug in the spring of 1944.

Mum and I evacuated again to stay with Peggy and her mother in Shropshire.

Dad and Nin stayed behind while the bungalow was repaired by the Council.

When we returned I remember many convoys of troops travelling down the by- pass nose to tail to the south coast to take part in the D-Day landings.

Whenever they stopped, Mum would take out refreshments and wish them luck. We also saw many aircraft and gliders flying south at nighttime.

In the summer of 1945 we prepared to come home. Dad came first to look for accommodation and found a flat over a shop called "The Pagoda" in Colomberie and a bit later we moved to a nearby house called "Eton Lodge" and started to set up home all over again.

"Crediton" was now occupied by one of the landlord's family which was fair enough but unforgivably, in my opinion, the landlord had taken all my family's possessions including jewellery and personal items 'in lieu of rent'.

I attended St James Street Primary School and thanks to a very strict dedicated head mistress called Grace Le Roux I passed a States Scholarship in 1947 to Jersey College for Girls. I also joined St Mark's Brownies and Guides.

When I think of what my family suffered I feel very sad. Their contribution to the war effort, quiet determination and courage is a lesson to us all. I am very proud of them.

Grief is the price we pay for love.

Eve with her mother left and with her family below

THE MEMORIES OF JOHN WAKEHAM

My family came to Jersey from Cardiff in 1930 when I was one year old, as my father had taken a job with Jersey Airways. At that time the planes were landing on the beach at West Park when the tide was out and it was not until 1937 that Jersey had an airport. My father drove the dowser or petrol tanker, and helped refuel the aircraft and generally helped with loading, etc; in those days everybody helped each other until the airport opened, when everything became more formal and he had to wear a uniform and gained the title of Refuelling Officer.

With the Germans taking over Paris, the States were advised by London that the Islands would not be defended, and they withdrew the Governor and all the British troops on the 21 June, 1940

As a young lad, I never thought that we would be invaded or beaten by the Germans; all the boys and girls believed that the British Empire was the best and strongest in the world. When the war began to go badly for us, we would hear the grown-ups talking about defeats and disasters but this did not have much effect on us, as we were British and would win by natural law – just like that.

So when my father was telling my mother one evening that Jersey Airways were offering to fly families out of the Island if they wished, I really did not understand, although when I asked questions I was reassured and told that there was no need to worry. In fact I thought it would be a good idea to go and visit relatives for a few weeks…. with no idea that the visit would last for five years.

A few days later it was all arranged. My cousin Reg, my mother and myself would fly off and go to our relatives in Wales.

Dad, of course, would have to stay until all the passengers had left, and then he too would leave and join us. This, however, was not to be as Jersey Airways were unable to keep a plane in Jersey on stand-by for the volunteers, and Dad was unable to leave the Island. In 1942 he was deported to Laufen and was eventually freed by the Americans. When he explained to them that he had been involved with aircraft, they took him to an airfield and he was sent back to England. On arrival there, he sent a telegram to his family to say he would be arriving the next morning.

When we arrived in England, my mother and her two boys were left to our own devices, and we made our way to our relatives in Wales. I do not know how my mother existed, she had very little money and had two lads to look after. Various people would take us in for a few days now and then.

Of course we had no news from Jersey, heard nothing from my father and only heard war news on the radio or in the newspapers. I remember my mother taking us up to London and going to the Houses of Parliament where we met Lord Portsea who took a great deal of interest in the affairs of the Channel Islanders and promised to look into our problems, but as far as I know we did not receive any other help.

However, eventually my mother did get work in an aircraft factory and I was sent to stay with an uncle and aunt in Clapton in Somerset. While I was there I had my 11th birthday on 15 September 1940 which was also, of course, the culmination of the Battle of Britain. I will never forget sitting on the grassy bank with a friend, Dennis Power, and his little sister watching the dogfights overhead. The sky was a mass of vapour trails while the engines roared and screamed and the sound of machine gunfire was everywhere. We watched many planes plummeting down without being able to tell whether they were friend or foe, neither were we aware of the importance of what we were seeing.

When we went home we did see a Heinkel which had crashed in a field, and we went over to it hoping to find a souvenir or two, but some troops - who I think were the Home Guard – came up and told us to go away. We did think that they were jolly mean!

From then on we seemed to be always on the move, and I started at many strange schools and met many new people. Of course, we received a good deal of sympathy, but there were times I became aware of hostility from adults as well as children, and I wonder if any other evacuees experienced this. As time went on I met other children from London and other parts of the United Kingdom and realized that many of them were suffering ill-treatment although others only received kindness.

I do remember being asked where I came from and found that very few of them knew anything about Jersey or the Channel Islands. When I tried to explain that Jersey was a small Island off the French coast in the bay of St Malo, I was regularly told that I was not British but French, and that we (the French) had betrayed the British and "run away" at Dunkirk. I did come in for some bullying as a consequence of this attitude, and became known as 'Frenchie'. In fact this nickname was with me when I started doing war work after leaving school in Wales. When we were living in a mountain village called Gwaelod-y-Garth I was even told I had a 'posh' upper class accent and, as many Welsh people then (and now) were very anti-English, I received some kicks and punches because of that. Even when I returned to Jersey (because by then I had a Welsh accent) quite a lot of people here called me Taffy and I was told I had run away from Jersey to save my skin, despite having done war work and been bombed. 'Twas ever thus – I suppose.

In April 1945 the war was at last coming to a close. The Russian steamroller was flattening all before it on the Eastern Front, and despite some setbacks, the Western allies were pushing into Germany through Holland and Belgium, while Italy had already capitulated in the south. Everything started to have a dreamlike feeling to us and we were impatient for news of our friends, relatives and our homes in the Island.

As my father still had his job at Jersey Airways, we returned to the Island just a few days after the Liberation.

THE MEMORIES OF MARJORIE ANNE BULL née LE COUTEUR

I was born on 10 April 1936 so I was four years old when in June 1940 my family left the Island. There were five of us – my mother, older brother Walter (six), myself at four, my younger brother Desmond who was three and our 22 month old sister Joyce. We departed on one of the last coal boats and were all down in the hold – a climb down by a steep ladder. On arrival in Britain we were all sent to the north of England and stayed at first in a large warehouse. Each family group were allocated one camp bed and how my mother and four children managed to sleep I will never know. Soon afterwards we were allocated a house at 6 Goldfinch Drive, Bury, which was a newly built estate where a number of houses were provided to evacuees. It was a quiet area in those days and we used to play in the street as we very rarely saw any cars. Milk was delivered by horse and cart each day.

I remember the air raid sirens going off quite frequently and we would all sleep in the cupboard under the stairs. There was an air raid shelter at the top of the street, but it had a direct hit and a number of lives were lost. Fortunately the houses either side of this shelter remained intact, but my mother would never take us to a shelter after that. There was a shelter in the school playground, and we always had to carry our gas masks with us.

My mother kept rabbits and grew vegetables in our garden, so rabbit stew would sometimes be on the menu. The skins were carefully dried and made into mittens and slippers for the whole family.

On Sundays we went to a Sunday School run by the Salvation Army, which was held in another Jersey family's home. They were a Mr and Mrs Hingston and my mother always said that they did a great deal to help all the evacuees in times of need; she was always very grateful to them.

Of course, during the winter when the snow was knee-deep we still went to school; we walked in the tracks made by vehicles. On the way to school we passed a sweet factory and my brother and his friends would shin up the pipes to get at the sticky substance oozing out at the top of them.

One summer our family went to St. Anne's-on-Sea near Blackpool and spent a lovely holiday at the seaside and I remember playing on the sand dunes and on the beach.

We all returned to Jersey in September 1945 and there was my father at the harbour waiting to greet us. Fortunately, our home was intact and the shed was full of chickens with rows of tobacco leaves hung up to dry. My grandparents lived next door and they had a lovely meal ready for us, followed by black grapes from the small lean-to greenhouse.

When we went to start school at First Tower School we were told there was no room for us and we would have to go to St. Aubin's School instead. My mother refused to send us there because of the cost of bus fares, etc. so we all enjoyed an extra month's holiday spent playing in Millbrook Park. Eventually we were allowed to start at First Tower School, although my teacher did not like my Lancashire accent and did her very best to change it!

THE MEMORIES OF MARY HEROLD née BLAMPIED

My childhood ended on a hot summer evening in June 1940; Our family lived in St Saviour's Road, and my Dad was Doctor H. J. Blampied. I was twelve years old when I said goodbye to my Dad, cat, dog and budgies and set sail at 5.00 p.m. from the Albert Pier on a very crowded mailboat with my Mum and her mother-in-law (my Gran) who was seventy- nine years old.

The deck was very crowded and once we had found a space on the floor no-one could move away. Gran was given a chair and we spent the entire long night huddled together. I had been made to wear layers of clothes including my winter coat, mackintosh and beret as Mum had said they would 'come in useful'. As usual, she was right! Those wretched clothes lasted for years and were then handed down to other evacuees – how I hated them!

The mailboat arrived at Southampton at 12.30 p.m. the next day having zigzagged across the channel to avoid minefields, German ships and planes. There was nothing to drink on the boat so we were not in good shape when we walked between barriers to confront the immigration officers. We were issued with identity numbers, but there was still no water. We eventually arrived at the railway platform where thankfully there was a tap.

We went on a train to Sherborne, Dorset and were driven to temporary accommodation in Acreman Street – just two attic rooms in a four storey house with poor Gran having to climb all those stairs. I was sent to school within two days of settling in and was the first evacuee to arrive so was welcomed with both kindness and curiosity. Later I was joined by girls from Poland, France, Denmark and Finland, so I was in good company but I missed my Jersey friends very much.

We spent August and September on a farm in Somerset where I learnt to hand milk a large herd of Shorthorn and Ayrshire cows with the land-girls who were replacing the men who had jointed the Forces. The cows were huge and I was frightened of them after the lovely little Jerseys. They all had horns in those days which made them look aggressive but I soon learnt that they were friendly.

The milk was bottled on the farm and I had to help deliver it in a milk float drawn by a very bad-tempered pony called Gypsy. There was one land-girl who had been a hairdresser and she was frightened of all animals and used to scream when the pony went backwards. It was really exciting with the rattling bottles and I held tight and loved it, and decided to be a milk girl for ever.

The village was full of evacuees from Portsmouth and Southampton and most of the boys worked on the farms both before and after school. Many hated it but a few loved the country life and stayed in Somerset all their lives.

Soon it was time for school again and Mum managed to rent a one bedroom flat with an attic and kitchen over a shop in the main street in Sherborne. The three of us squeezed in and even had Jersey friends to stay who were still homeless.

In August the Battle of Britain was at its peak and then the German planes began to attack towns and factories. Bristol and Yeovil were badly bombed and we used to hear the planes overhead after the air raid sirens had gone off. On 30 September thirty-seven Heinkel bombers flew over to attack the Westland factory at Yeovil. However clouds prevented them from seeing their target so they dropped all their bombs (three hundred or so) across Sherborne town. It was only 5.30 p.m. so people were out in the streets and many were killed. Albert Le Gallais, a Jerseyman, was among them and there is a memorial plaque in Half Moon Street by Sherborne Abbey, commemorating this event.

There was no "All clear" signal as there was no electricity, gas, telephone nor water services left. The streets were blocked with rubble and it was devastating to see the damage. Some unexploded bombs and the piles of rubble were removed by hand by teams of workmen. However things soon returned to normal with all helping each other. It was terrible when service men returned home on leave to find their families and homes were no longer there.

The winter of 1940 was a very grim one for us all and in 1941 I was very ill at the Yeatman Hospital with appendicitis. The Sherborne people were very supportive to Mum and Gran when I was 'on the brink'. There were no antibiotics then, just wonderful nursing. Various kind people came and read to me.

I enjoyed that and at last the day came when I was able to leave the hospital and I was told, "No school for you for one year".

Mum then rented a tiny thatched cottage in a village five miles from Sherborne which was very pretty (but bitterly cold) with one bedroom and one living room with a huge draughty fireplace. We were given two parcels of clothes by the Canadian Red Cross, with warm pullovers, woollen stockings, coats and hats and very huge thick blankets. We were all very grateful.

As I was getting better a friend from school gave me three Rhode Island Red pullets, so I had to register as a poultry keeper to get rations of balancer meal. With boiled up scraps and lots of care they laid well – so I was able to sell the eggs and had money to spend at last. The cottage had a big garden so I learnt to grow vegetables and to enjoy gardening.

Thus that one year passed quickly and I had to go back to school.

Eventually Mum found a small bungalow on a hill outside Sherborne which was to be our last home in England. It had a big garden where I grew vegetables and sunflower seeds; these I dried and then sent up to a lady who lived in Park Lane who owned a starving parrot. She was so grateful since she had had that bird for several years. Mum and I met her in London and she even came to Jersey after the war to thank me again.

My Gran died when she was 81. She never returned home and I missed her very much. Gran had never grumbled and she managed all the wartime restrictions with a wonderful spirit. She made many friends in Dorset but was sad to have been torn away from her only son, her home and the sea.

The Red Cross letters were a blessing but they took months to arrive and were often returned with big holes cut out by the censors' scissors. We were allowed only twenty five words a letter and they were very difficult to write. We were always worried about Dad and our relatives and the worst thing was the unknown.

My brother, Edward, joined the Navy at 17 in 1942, and was on HMS Norfolk in the Battle of the North Cape in the Artic seas when the German battlecruiser Scharnhorst was sunk. Then he was in charge of a M.F. (Motor Fire) Boat dealing with fires and explosions both before and after, as well as at, the D.Day landings. So Mum had plenty to worry about.

Mum taught at Sherborne Boys Prep School after all the masters had joined up. Despite having no qualifications she managed very well.

When the Belsen concengtration camp was liberated in April 1945 and the full horrors exposed, we were desperately worried for all the Channel Islanders who had been sent to Europe. We did not feel one hundred per cent happy until we heard the broadcast from Winston Churchill that 'our dear Channel Islands are also to be freed today'. At last the war in Europe was over and we had our Liberation Day, and now we could only think of when we would be home !

My brother returned first as he had hitched a passage on a naval ship to Guernsey and after spending the night there had a lift on an M.T.B. to St. Helier, where he stayed for two days with Dad before returning to the U.K. the same way.

We had some frustrating delays but in June we packed three suitcases, gave everything else to our wartime friends, and took the train to London. After spending one day there to get travel permits, tickets etc., we caught the Waterloo train to Southampton where the night boat was waiting. The Isle of Guernsey steamed down the Solent and was en route to the Channel Islands. Everyone was excited as this was the first mailboat to return after five long, hard years and as we arrived at St Peter Port in Guernsey we heard cheering across the water with the Guernsey people welcoming us all back home. They were standing along the road by the old Woolworth store and were not allowed to come any closer. Emotions were high – with both cheering and crying in the dawn light.

After unloading we steamed through the pier heads where I saw my first Germans; they were prisoners who were knocking down a gun emplacement. I think we must have had some breakfast but perhaps we were too excited to eat. First Grosnez then La Rocco Tower and then dear Corbiere lighthouse were passed and it was a shock to see all the German defences and towers as we had had no warnings of this and I was stunned by the great gun at Noirmont. Then we were crossing St Aubin's Bay in bright sunshine and with the Isle dressed overall in flags and bunting, we entered St Helier Harbour.

What a welcome we received – crowds and crowds of people standing and cheering on the upper wall of the Albert Pier stretching down to the abattoirs. We had to go through Immigration which was set up in the bar, then out on deck to be greeted by the Bailiff with a kiss and hug, and shook hands with States members.

Coming down the gang plank I heard my name being called. "Mary! Mary!" And there were some of my old school friends to welcome us. My Mum was the first passenger to step back on to Jersey soil, and I was the second.

It was wonderful – but where was my Dad? We found him further down the pier and no words can express the joy we felt on seeing him. I had left Jersey at 12 years old and returned at 17 – what a dreadful time to be away from my Island.

I would not like to repeat those years, but I will always be grateful to my parents who gave up so much to enable me to grow up in freedom. I would also like to thank the kindness and friendship of those I met while in exile.

Mary with the sunflowers she grew for feeding the parrot

THE MEMORIES OF TERRY GAUDIN

I was 15 years old and at school (The Beeches) on 19 June 1940 and there was an odd feeling in town since many soldiers had arrived from St Malo and were staying at the Merton Hotel, while the gorse on Fort Regent was burning.

However, with only an hour's notice our party of 12 people managed to get on the ss Archangel on Thursday 20 June. With my mother and father and me, were my mother's sister and her husband, Olga and Cecil Blight, my father's two sisters Elsie and her husband Eddie Carter, and Gracie and her husband Cyril Noble, the latter being a well known local singer. Cyril Noble's seventy year old mother was also in the party together with Edna Harris the daughter of my mother's brother who was 16.

We travelled overnight and made ourselves comfortable as best we could; drinking water was very scarce and on our way to Weymouth a warship came close and advised the captain to go to Southampton, where on landing we went to an ice rink where there were refreshments for us but no bedding.

On a point of interest, ss Archangel was a ferry boat and was apparently one of the first boats to arrive at Dunkirk. She had a hand grenade launcher installed on her stern.

The next day we were taken to the railway station and there our large party split up and my parents and I went to London since my mother had two sisters living in Southall, Middlesex.

By 1 August I had a job where I earned 18shillings and nine pence a week, and we also had our first air-raid warning. Some weeks later I got a job at Hayes with HMV.

We were able to rent an empty house in a street of 150 houses and we moved some furniture in but as the gas cooker was not yet connected we went back to my aunt's house. That night a bombing raid destroyed both houses. When I was at work and the air-raid warning sounded, all the staff went to two fields filled with shelters, one field being reached by crossing a canal bridge and pontoon.

As no work was being done it was decided that the staff would have a spotter on the roof of the building to give a warning and we ignored the public system. Eventually five storey shelters were built in the angle of the main building and fire fighting parties were organized overnight.

Then it was the turn of the V1 flying bomb which arrived day and night; these could be seen as they flew low and sounded like motor cycles, but when the engine stopped they came down and exploded. One landed on the single storey shelter of my factory, blowing all the walls out and dropping the roof on to 37 people.

These raids continued until six weeks before the end of the war, when the V2 rockets started. These gave no warning and when they came down and made holes big enough to put a bus in !

With the European war ending came the possibility of returning home to Jersey. As I was in a reserved occupation I could not be called up and although I wanted to be home for Christmas 1945, I did not arrive until the New Year. Sadly four of my family died during the war.

Terry Gaudin and family

THE STORY OF NELLIE LEBREDONCHEL née Hotton

My name was Nelley Hotton, and I was five and a half years old when I lived with my mum, dad and two sisters – Joan aged four and a half and Margaret eight months old – at Beaumont, St Peter, in June 1940.

At the time, my baby sister was ill in hospital and Mum had to walk with my other sister and me to the hospital every day to visit her. One particular day, Matron told my mother that all the patients were being sent home as the authorities did not know what would happen when the Germans arrived. According to Mum, she was told to go and get a pram, and then go into the Town Hall to collect the papers to get on a ship to be evacuated from Jersey.

Mum did this while Dad was at work. She was then only 23 years old, had never left Jersey and the furthest she had travelled was to Corbiere from St Peter. There was no way Mum could contact Dad, as he worked for Mr Poigndestre at First Tower doing deliveries, and in the afternoons he had a milk round to carry out.

Having obtained a pram, Mum then walked back to Beaumont leaving my sister in the Hospital, and began to put a few things together to take with us taking, as advised by the Matron, mostly things for the baby.

Then we all walked back to the Hospital the next day, collected Margaret and walked down o the Albert Pier, where the queue was almost as long as the whole length of the pier.

The boat itself was very crowded and once Mum and we three children found a space, we were told to stay where we were and we were the only passengers to have a pram. Eventually, we heard Dad talking to my Uncle and so we were re-united. I believe that the boat we were on was ss Archangel.

As we were nearing Southampton, my mother was asked to throw the new pram overboard ! This was because the crew wanted to dismantle the decking to use for fuel. Mum told us to hold on to her very tightly as we could see the sea below us.

Apparently we were told first of all that we were supposed to go to a stadium once we arrived, but that was changed and instead we were all put on to a train, which did not move and we stayed in the safety of a tunnel overnight. In the morning, when we left the train we found that the stadium had been burnt to the ground overnight – it must have been bombed! We were then taken off to some big shed (I do remember that) and all the women had to have a medical because the authorities wanted them to join up. Mum did not pass this medical as she discovered she was pregnant, whilst my father who had poor eye-sight, also did not pass.

Once we had this news, the four of us were put onto another train which went to Barnsley, which was to be our future home. However, once we arrived at Barnsley the family went to live in the hospital as Margaret was still sick, and we stayed until Dad found us a house, when we still had to leave Margaret in the hospital.

Dad had found a job in a factory that made briquettes for fires; there was no work in Barnsley so he worked in both Sheffield and Wakefield. All the other evacuees who had been with us were allocated homes, but as we were in the hospital it was left to Dad to find a property for us when we finally left there. He did find us a house although he struggled to find furniture for it.

Unfortunately Mum was unable to work not only because of my sister, but also because she was expecting her baby; she was told that she had to put up another family of evacuees, in this case a mother and her four grown up girls. It was a tight squeeze!

As we were now settled, I went to St Mary's School. One day the Inspector arrived and told me that I had not attended school for that term. The reason was that when the teacher called the register she could not pronounce my name and so I had never answered. I do not remember having any school holidays.

The other children would ask if I found it strange being in school clothes, as they thought we wore raffia skirts and tiny tops; they thought we had come from the Caribbean.

In February 1941 my brother Donald was born, and thankfully not long after that Margaret finally came home from hospital. We only had one gas ring to warm up the food to give to Donald.

My mother took us all for the christening of Donald to a church to which all the evacuees went. It even had a Jersey flag outside. As it was usual to have the baptisms on a Sunday afternoon there were other families having their own children christened at the same time. Mostly there were no fathers present as they were away elsewhere ether fighting or working. Everyone got to know one another after the service and we went to Lockward Park where the children could run around and play. A treat was half a jam sandwich at the end of the afternoon.

Mum used to take we children for a walk every Sunday afternoon to try to find the sea! But of course we never did so as it was so far away.

While we were in England, two other brothers were born, Raymond and Ted. I used to tell them stories about our real home in Jersey, and promised them that one day they would be able to play on the beach.

In 1945 we were told that at last Jersey had been liberated, and that we could go home. We caught a train to Southampton and then finally found ourselves on a boat ready to sail home. My two younger brothers did not know what was happening as they were too small, but I remember that they cried a lot.

My grandfather was working as a docker when the boat arrived at the Albert Pier and he was overjoyed when he saw Mum and Dad coming down the gangway; he was not so pleased when he saw her with a baby in her arms. At first he did not realize that the baby was his grandson, and then he saw two more boys holding on to my mother's coat and on to me.

Mum went away with three girls, and came back with them and three boys...

We all stayed at the Gloucester Hotel with other returning evacuees so Dad could get our house in order. To do this, Dad, my sisters and I walked from the Hotel to Beaumont every day to get everything ready before we all moved back into our home.

One of the conditions of being allowed back into the Island, was that Dad had to have a job to do. Soon Dad was working for the States of Jersey taking up the sleepers from the German railway line which they had laid from West Park to Corbiere.

THE WAR MEMORIES OF BILL BLAMPIED

My mother was Doris Maud Cousins and she was born in Guernsey. My father was Edwin Blampied and met my mother in Guernsey during a holiday over there. They married in 1928 and lived at Pulwake Villas in Aubin Lane, Bagot.

Dad's best friend was Guernseyman Bert Harris who lived next door and they both worked for Mr Wakeham at Bashfords Nurseries, building greenhouses for years.

Dad joined the Royal Artillery and with other Islanders went to war, he survived and returned in 1945.

I was just three months short of my sixth birthday and clearly remember leaving the Island with my mother, brothers Ron (eleven), Eric (nine), Michael (five) and Brian (three) plus sisters Gladys (seven) and Joan (four). My Aunty Dolly and seven cousins were also leaving with us.

I have a lasting memory of being in the hull of a coal boat and looking up and seeing the blue sky through the hatch.

We docked at Southampton and then had a 13 hour train journey to Burnley. My cousin Rose Heath (née Hairon) reminded me that the volunteer services offered passengers food and drink when the train stopped at stations along the way. At that time we would have been overjoyed at their kindness.

We all stayed for two weeks at Burch Hill Hospital in Burnley. I can remember how the sirens would alert us to make our way down to the basement of the hospital. To get there we had to go down the steel staircase on the outside of the building in the darkness which was very frightening for all of us. I still get a strange feeling when I hear any sirens wailing now.

From Burch Hill we were moved to Eastwood near Todmorden. We lived in an old shop until the end of the war.

For the first few days the younger children, myself and two sisters slept in the shop drawers with blankets and pillows. My mother and two older brothers slept upstairs on mattresses on the floor. Within days people arrived with furniture and household items to make it feel more like a home, which was very kind of them.

Aunty Dolly and my cousins moved to Shoreclough in Rochdale and we would travel to stay with them during our school summer holidays. During one visit, when I was about nine years old, I went with Rose to the first ever Co-Operative shop to be opened in Toad Lane, Rochdale.

I can clearly recall hearing and seeing doodlebugs passing over Eastwood. Thank goodness they all passed over and fell on the moors. I can also vividly remember seeing many formations of planes overhead.

We left England and arrived back in Jersey during September 1945 to be met by my aunt and uncle (Herbert and Olga Blampied) who lived at First Tower. It took my uncle a couple of trips in his car to take us all back to their home, and on the way to their home we spotted our famous name "Blampied Stores".

We stayed at their home for two weeks as our home was being lived in by another family at that time and we moved back to 3 Pulwake Villas which belonged to Dad's employer Mr Wakeham and for whom my dad continued working after the war.

Another memory is that when I was 11 years old, I was pushing a hand cart with my two brothers Ron and Derek. The cart was filled with suitcases and our belongings and we were pushing it from First Tower to Bagot Road.

As we were going down Don Road we lost control of the cart and it went crashing in to the wall. With kind help from passers-by we managed to get back to Pulwake Villas, where the family lived for many years to come.

THE EVACUATION FROM JERSEY OF
PEARL E. WALTON née Colls

We decided to leave Jersey on 17 June 1940 and spent a worrying and frantic day deciding what to take and what not to take. We had a comfortable crossing on the boat and were lucky, as some friends of ours had to make the journey to England in the hold of a coal boat and they had to leave everything behind.

On arrival at Southampton we saw, for the first time, barrage balloons. This seemed to be the beginning of a fantastic dream; there was tenseness in the air and in the faces of the people. I think they had had their first air raid the day before. Soldiers returning from Dunkirk were everywhere.

There was little or no help to be had on the stations. Unfortunately, in my haste I had packed baby Adrian's bottle, Cow and Gate and his other necessities in a paper bag. This, of course, burst at the worst possible moment when we were struggling with cases, coats and baby.

After a long and exhausting journey, we arrived at Dynas Powis, South Wales, between Berry and Cardiff. As you can imagine, this was not the best of places during a war and the sirens sounded on our first night. I shall never forget that first time. It sent a cold shiver down my spine. We leapt out of bed almost asleep, grabbed Adrian and made for the cellars. Our bedroom was at the top of a three storey house and it trembled with the force of the explosions. Five bombs were dropped, two of them very close to the house and some of the windows were broken – but we were lucky !

Another night – or should I say early morning – about thirty bombs were dropped in our district. I remember the wonderful feeling of relief when the 'All Clear' was sounded, and also those wonderful cups of tea brewed in the early hours.

A few months later we moved to Penarth, a short distance from Cardiff, and an equally bad spot as far as bombing was concerned. We had some large guns near us, and if we happened to be nearby when they fired, they made us nearly jump out of our skin with their 'swishing' noise. Sometimes, the siren would sound when we were in town shopping, and this was not a pleasant experience especially with a small child.

I found myself in those days becoming a bit absent minded. One day I purchased my rations, walked a quarter of the way home, and then suddenly realised that I had left something behind. . Good heavens… THE BABY!

Back I rushed to the shop to find him still playing happily in his pram.

In March 1941 Penarth had a severe blitz; people were killed and a couple of churches burnt down. We seemed to be surrounded by fires caused by incendiary bombs and the whole town was lit up with flares dropped by the planes.

Many nights were spent lying under a steel shutter, but one night stands out in my memory – the sight of a neighbour with a vegetable strainer stuck on her head !

Martin arrived in 1944, and I would like to state here that never have I seen such healthy babies as those born in the war. Maybe it was because we were stuffed with vitamin pills and whatnot.

VE Day, 8 May 1945, came at last and we celebrated with large bonfires, burning dummies of Hitler and with flags everywhere.

Two months later was VJ Day, 15 August 1945, when we heard that Japan had accepted surrender terms. Again there were tea parties for the children, bonfires and flags.

I think one fact emerges from the whirlpool of events during these years; the spirit of friendly co-operation amongst the people. If this spirit could only prevail during the years of peace, how very much happier everyone would be.

Athelstan, Adrian and Pearl Walton, Cardiff 1941

190

A SPECIAL HEIRLOOM LEAVES THE ISLAND

The history of Jersey shows that it has occupied a special place in Royal affections and has enjoyed this privilege for many centuries. That Jersey remained an English possession of the King of England after the Crown lands in France were lost more 800 years ago, doubtless accounts for part of this mutual fondness.

The bond was, however, reinforced tremendously during the English Civil War. Jersey remained as a centre of Royalist resistance and became a refuge for the future kings Charles II and James II when the Royalist cause of their father, King Charles I, was lost.

When the de Carteret family from St Ouen's Manor left the Island in 1940, the mother of the present Seigneur of the Manor took with her possibly the most famous heirloom from the Manor. This was a letter from King Charles II thanking the de Carteret family for their aid to him during the English Civil War.

Sources : The internet and Mr Howard Baker

BOYS FROM VICTORIA COLLEGE EVACUATED
TO BEDFORD SCHOOL

During August 1940, College House, the boarding house attached to Victoria College became the headquarters of the Feldkommandantur 515 (Field Command 515) of the occupying German forces.

The College itself was commandeered for the Reichsarbeitsdienst (German Labour Service) and housed members of the Hitler Youth and, after 1941, forced labourers of the Organisation Todt who had been brought to Jersey to build fortifications. The staff and pupils were evacuated to Halkett Place Elementary School in St Helier under the headmastership of Mr P.A. Tatam although some 40 boys, their parents and several members of staff evacuated to Bedford School in June 1940 for the duration of the German Occupation. The Victoria College teaching staff at Bedford were Mr J.H. Grummitt, Mr Hopewell and Miss Aubrey. Although the boys and staff were assimilated into Bedford School they maintained their own identity of 'Victoria College at Bedford',under the headmastership of Mr S.M. Toyne. Mr Toyne was the retired headmaster of St Peter's School in York and had acted at Bedford School in a part-time capacity.

In the Liberation edition of the 'Victoria College at Bedford School' newsletter published in July 1945, Mr Toyne wrote: "Firstly allow me to express the joy and thankfulness which were felt in Bedford when we learned of the liberation of the Island. Secondly we should like members of Victoria College, Jersey, to know that at each of our Sunday meetings prayers were offered for their welfare and safety. Victorians in Jersey can rest assured that the traditions in work and games have been well maintained. Not only in Higher and School Certificates have the successes been most gratifying, but besides the University Scholarships won by Durell and d'Authreau at Oxford and Cambridge, a really brilliant series of Oxford and State Scholarships has crowned Benest's successful career at Bedford School. In athletics including rowing, Victorians have done well and we must congratulate G. Thorn on playing for the 1st XI at cricket.

"The general success of the venture could not have been attained had it not been for the wholehearted support of the Headmaster of Bedford, Mr Grose Hodge, and the open-hearted hospitality of the Bedford masters and boys."

'Victoria College at Bedford' even maintained its own Board of Governors; Old Victorians Lord Justice du Parcq and Messrs C.T. Le Quesne, Guy Malet de Carteret and Ralph Vibert.

On 23 May 1945, the Bailiff of Jersey, Mr Alexander Coutanche, wrote a Liberation Message to the evacuated Victorians at Bedford School. In that letter he wrote: "In the past few days (since the Liberation on 9 May) so many hands have been outstretched to help us, so much material assistance has been lavished upon us, so many sacred ties with our kinfolk overseas have been renewed, that it is impossible to write any words which would be adequate to the occasion. That we are all overjoyed is obvious, that our hearts are overflowing with emotion is a confession which every one of us will gladly make, that we are profoundly grateful is an understatement. In our isolation, we have thought of you and prayed for you. We have profoundly admired your gallantry and your great achievements. That together we may rebuild our life is our one desire. God bless you all – and thank you."

Most Victorians and their parents returned to Jersey in July and August 1945 although both Mr Grummitt and Mr Hopewell had moved to new appointments in schools and colleges in Britain.

Strong links are still maintained by Victoria College with Bedford School and in 2008 Bedford School donated a number of magnificent chandeliers to the College which today grace the Great Hall. In May 2009, the play 'Dear Channel Islanders', written by Old Victorian Peter Tabb, was performed at Bedford School by boys of Victoria College as a major event in the inaugural Bedford-Jersey Arts Festival.

EVACUATION FROM ST MALO

It was on Monday morning 17 June 1940 that there was a call for volunteers to take their boats to St Malo at once for dangerous work and we quickly got together a crew of three to man our small 30ft boat. The boat had been laid up since April and we got to work immediately and got ready for sea. We were given orders to leave at 10.00 pm and together with about eight other small craft we set sail. It was a lovely moon-lit night and we kept on deck all the way.

We arrived at dawn at St Malo and reported to the naval commander in charge whose job it was to take the demolition party off. He asked our word of honour to be about 15 kilometres away. He gave us money to go into the town and have breakfast. It was an inspiration to see the coolness of the sailors left to do the demolition.

At the hotel we met three soldiers who had missed the boat at Cherbourg and after overrunning a German mechanized unit, eventually arrived at St Malo. They were told by a captain to keep with us as that was their last chance to get away.

After a good feed we found our way to the docks and about 2.25 pm a huge blaze lit the sky and we had to stand by.

We could plainly see the commander and the sailors setting the fuses and one by one the explosions went off and we saw whole steel plates blown 500 ft in the air. The lock towers went off next. The explosions were terrific and we had to hold on. After each charge went off we could see the commander going over to see the job was done properly. We were now on the alert as the Germans were reported on the outskirts of the town. Bren guns were set up on our decks. After the last lorries were thrown into the harbour and everything which might be useful to the enemy was destroyed, the commander got everyone aboard our small craft and we set sail. We were the last boat to leave and we left St Malo dock a blazing ruin.

Our return journey was different. We encountered heavy seas and as dusk fell our engines failed after we had shipped a huge wave and we have to rely on sail. Night was falling and we all worked hours trying to get our engine going. As it was blowing half a gale we heaved to and let the boat drift all night taking turns keeping the watch.

Some of the sailors we had picked up were tired out and fell fast asleep. We could see St Malo blazing from 12 miles away.

Before dawn we hoisted sail but the going was difficult as we had a head wind. We sailed for hours and eventually found ourselves near the Minquiers and narrowly missed a rock by only 15ft with the wind drifting us on to it.

We could plainly see Jersey at last and were overtaken by a Belgian boat with French and Polish soldiers. They had come from Dinard. They took us in tow and we arrived at St Helier on Wednesday evening 19 June 1940 only to find that the life boat was out looking for us.

From an account written by Mr. W. P. Williams, source G.O. Evacuation Escape Box No 2, Société Jersiaise Library

A BRIEF HISTORY OF THE GERMAN OCCUPATION OF JERSEY
1940 to 1945
What the evacuees would have faced had they stayed
by Peter Tabb
Author of 'A Peculiar Occupation'

On 20 June 1940, with France subdued, Germany's architects of blitzkreig gave the order to their forward commanders: "The capture of the British Channel Islands is necessary and urgent."

By 1 July the Channel Islands were in German hands, under foreign dominion for the first time in more than a thousand years. Operation Green Arrows had been a success.

The subsequent occupation of Jersey by German forces during the Second World War lasted almost five years and, like invaders down the centuries, the occupiers left an indelible mark, not just on the Island's history but also on its landscape. That the Channel Islands were the only British soil to be occupied by German forces gave the invaders, in their estimation, a valuable propaganda tool. But it was not until October 1941, more than 15 months after the invasion, that the order was given, a Führerbefehl from Adolf Hitler himself, that the Islands were to be converted into 'impregnable fortresses'.

The fortification process he instigated would last until early 1944 and consume ten per cent of all the concrete used to construct the Atlantikmaur, the 'Atlantic Wall', that stretched from the North Cape of Norway to the Spanish border.

It is little wonder that, looking back to the long sunny summer of 1940, many still ask why and how the Islands came to be invaded.

In 1933 Adolf Hitler and the Nazi Party came to power in Germany by democratic means but within just a year Hitler had demolished the democratic apparatus that had conferred that power upon him. The Nazi Party's desire for lebensraum, living space, for the German people brought Hitler into conflict with the other major European powers and following the German invasion of Poland in September 1939, much of the world found itself again at war, just 20 years after the end of the war that was to have ended all wars.

By June 1940, Germany had invaded and occupied Denmark, Norway, Holland, Belgium and France and was poised to cross the English Channel to invade Britain. In the Bay of St Malo, just 14 miles from the French coast, the British Channel Islands lay undefended. To the German commanders their capture was 'necessary and urgent' since, unless taken, the Islands could pose a threat to German plans to create U-boat bases on France's Atlantic coast, dominating as they do, the Western Approaches to the English Channel.

The likely German plans were not unknown to the British Government nor to the Island authorities and the evacuation of all military personnel (the small, lightly armed garrison had posed no threat to the triumphant German panzers who had just defeated entire British, French and Belgian armies) and civilians followed; about a tenth of Jersey's population and almost half from Guernsey opting for the unknown of a new life in war-torn Britain. Many young men had already volunteered for military service (the Islands had never been subject to conscription). Those left behind braced themselves for invasion.

Sadly the British authorities failed to advise the Germans that the Islands had been demilitarised and were undefended (it being perceived that this was tantamount to inviting the Germans to invade) and on 28 June German Heinkel HE111 aircraft bombed and machine-gunned the Islands' ports, apparently in the mistaken belief that the lorries there filled with produce for export (something of a forlorn hope) were loaded with military equipment! Forty-four Islanders were killed.

The way was now open for uncontested occupation. It was not long in coming.

Being sea-girt, the capture of the Channel Islands was to have been the responsibility of the Kriegsmarine, the German Navy. However, the glory of taking the Islands, if that is what it was, fell to pilots of the Luftwaffe, the air force. In Guernsey Hauptmann Liebe-Pieteritz and in Jersey Oberleutnant Kern landed at the Islands' respective airports and found local dignitaries prepared to surrender to them, the terms dropped in linen bags earlier having been accepted by the authorities who, without guidance from the British Home Office, had to cope with the tragedy of potential occupation as best they could.

On 1 July the German Navy arrived, bringing troops of the 319 Infantry Division who had recently fought their way across Europe. Soldiers immediately occupied the Town Hall and Post Office in Jersey and Government House in Guernsey. Within two days German forces had also landed on Alderney, already almost totally evacuated, and also Sark where the redoubtable Dame (a fluent German speaker) greeted the occupiers as unexpected, uninvited and hopefully very temporary guests.

In a matter of days, 150 square miles of British territory has been successfully invaded and occupied, without the loss of a single man, for the first time since the Middle Ages.

For many of the occupiers, exploring wide-eyed islands that only a matter of days before had still been welcoming summer visitors, the well-stocked shops, the comfortable hotels and the wary but polite local population implied that a similar invasion of mainland Britain (where not a few already thought they were) could well be a similar walkover.

Those first few weeks of occupation seemed unreal to both occupier and occupied alike. The Islanders were gratified to discover that the invaders were invariably polite, well disciplined and were even prepared to take their place in the inevitable queues that formed at the local shops and pay cash for the goods they required. Many of the occupiers spoke good English and clearly intended to prove that they were not at all the barbarians who had been reported as having rampaged across Europe. For the invaders there were surprises too. Hitherto they had been used to authorities fleeing and leaving just chaos behind. In the Islands the infrastructure survived, the Islands' governments still functioned, the local police forces still controlled the traffic and investigated crime and the civilian heads of population made it clear that their people would look to them, not the Germans, for governance.

Initially the 2000 or so invaders took over empty hotels and houses for their accommodation and most Islanders were actually little disturbed by their presence. Nevertheless the ubiquity of the Germans could not be ignored. Every day notices detailing new restrictions appeared in the local press, particularly as supplies in the shops dwindled. A curfew and blackout were imposed and staples which had always been taken for granted, particularly motor fuel and coal, began very quickly to be in short supply. Islanders were instructed to drive on the right (with the inevitable casualties) and the reduction in supplies of petrol meant that Islanders took to two wheels rather than four, particularly as most privately-owned vehicles were arbitrarily requisitioned for military use. The invaders' gleeful buying up of shop goods that they had not seen for months or even years (like talcum powder, scented soap, silk stockings and underwear for their wives and girlfriends at home) meant that many shops ran out of stock very quickly with no hope of re-supply. Indeed Woolworths, always one of St Helier's busiest stores, closed within six months and was not to re-open until after the Liberation.

The German propaganda machine was busy too; pictures of German soldiers conversing with 'British' policemen and a German soldier buying a 'Smiths London ice cream' were sent home and published as proof that parts of Britain itself had already fallen under German hegemony and indeed the invaders were gazing on a much bigger quarry just 90 miles over the northern horizon.

However, after September 1940, the Islanders glumly realised that their invaders, their grandiose plans for invading Britain by dominating the skies having been so effectively thwarted by the Royal Air Force, were now likely to cling even more tenaciously to the few pieces of British soil they already had.

Thus the occupation began in earnest and things really did begin to change.

At the time of the invasion in July 1940 the population of Jersey was around 45,000 people and that of Guernsey around 20,000. The initial German garrisons were small, less than 2,000 men in each major island, and much smaller groups in Alderney and Sark. The occupiers' numbers remained largely unchanged for more than a year, the anticipated raids by a Britain eager to reclaim its offshore possessions never materialising (except for a few 'pinpricks' which were for intelligence gathering purposes only and were mostly farcical failures).

Initially the administration of the Islands was in the hands of the Wehrmacht, the German military. Within weeks of the invasion, to cope with the new circumstances, the States of Jersey had appointed a Superior Council to run local affairs and a similar body in Guernsey, the Controlling Committee, was also formed. These bodies were headed by the Bailiff (the Island's civilian head and an office that can trace its ancestry back to

William the Conqueror), the principal Law Officers (who were all British Crown appointments) and the heads of established government departments who were mostly elected politicians.

Within two months the Germans set up a new command structure with the Islands being administered by Feldkommandantur 515, responsible for all civilian affairs and itself being subject to the overall control of the Islands' military command (the Festungkommandantur) who would direct matters were the islands ever to be invaded. The men and few women who comprised FK 515 were mostly civilians in uniform, civil servants and bureaucrats drafted to the Islands from Germany. Most spoke good English.

From the outset the occupation of the Channel Islands was to be more than a simple military exercise run by soldiers. A civilian/military bureaucracy was created that, with its complexity, could have run an entire country rather than a group of small islands. These bodies interested themselves in every aspect of Island life including price control, policing, education (teaching the German language became mandatory in schools), health, postal services and the rationing of food and essential supplies and doing things very much in their own way.

After the war Jersey's Bailiff, Alexander Coutanche, when asked how he coped with the constant stream of orders and instructions (which often countermanded each other) that emanated from Feldkommandantur 515, replied simply, "I protested." And he kept protesting to the very last day of the war. It is perhaps to the credit of the men and women of FK 515, many of whom had legalistic backgrounds, that because they believed they were acting within international law and had wanted to create 'a model occupation', many of his protests were actually taken note of and acted upon.

Life began to develop a bleak pattern, one categorised mostly by boredom as pre-war pursuits became more and more difficult to follow. Cinemas closed for lack of films. Libraries received no stocks of new books. Listening to the radio was soon banned since the BBC had the nasty habit of broadcasting news that the Germans did not want anyone to hear. The curfew meant that visiting friends was strictly a limited day-time activity. Organisations like the Salvation Army, the Royal Jersey Golf Club, the Scouts and St John's Ambulance and even the Girls Friendly Society were banned. Everyday items like tobacco became in short supply, the Islanders putting matches to such substitutes as dried blackberry leaves, dock leaves and even used tea leaves. English money disappeared (largely because many Germans sent the British coinage home as souvenirs) to be replaced by the reichsmark, worth a little over 10p. Prices, and wages, were fixed.

While the maintenance of law and order was still largely in the hands of the civilian police and the Jersey courts, alongside them there was the sinister presence of the Geheimefeldpolizei, literally the Secret Field Police, whose role it was to quell any political opposition to their version of good order. The Gfp had originally been part of the Abwehr, the military intelligence service under the control of the Wehrmacht. Although in Jersey Islanders referred to the three man Gfp force as the Gestapo, the Channel Islands were spared the excesses of the security apparatus created and operated by the Nazi Party. The Gfp was augmented by the Feldgendarmerie and although the latter was a uniformed organisation whose presence was almost always betrayed by the clanking of their silver breastplates, their activities gave Islanders something of an insight into the kind of ruthless suppression of opposition practised by the truly dreaded Gestapo throughout the rest of occupied Europe and within Germany itself.

Although the Channel Islands had long been famous for their exports of potatoes, tomatoes and vegetables, the Islands had never actually been capable of feeding their own populations from their own resources and since all manufactured goods had always been imported (mostly from Britain) new ways had to be found to sustain the Islands' populations which ultimately included another 30,000 mouths needing to be fed. A Purchasing Commission was set up to trade with France, headed by the bi-lingual John Jouault for Jersey and Raymond Falla for Guernsey.

In the Islands barter became a common currency - a set of bicycle tyres being exchanged for five pounds of flour, for instance - and inevitably the black market reared its ugly head. At one time a pound of tea was selling for £30, or about three months' wages for a labourer, and a pound of tobacco for around £100, a whole year's wages for some.

In October 1941 fuel rationing was announced but also in that same month a Führerbefehl from Adolf Hitler commanded that the Islands be turned into 'impregnable fortresses'. He had decided that the Channel Islands should become Germany's Gibraltar, an outpost on the edge of Europe to be retained by the new owners in perpetuity.

Within weeks the German garrison in Jersey had swelled almost tenfold, to a full infantry division of 15,000 men. More hotels were requisitioned and private houses, even many still lived in by their owners, found new occupants.

Soon the Germans were building defences in earnest, digging trenches and knocking down buildings to create clear fields of fire. The Jersey railways, closed for many years, were reactivated to move building materials - sand, gravel and cement - rapidly to those areas where strongpoints and resistance nests were to be created. Narrow gauge railway lines were laid across private property and even through farmyards and gardens, linking docks, quarries and sandpits with the fortifications the materials they carried would build. Today these railways have entirely disappeared although the discerning can discover traces of their erstwhile busy existence.

The first defences were built by the Division's own pioneers but soon forced labourers of the Organisation Todt began making an appearance.

Initially these workers, recruited throughout occupied Europe, were mostly Frenchmen and Spaniards (former republicans who had fled to France only to be handed over to the Germans by a pliant Vichy government) and North Africans. They worked for the German civilian building contractors brought to the Island to turn Hitler's order into concrete reality.

These workers were fed and paid and the Germans also tried to recruit local tradesmen by offering wages well in excess of those they could earn from Island employers.

However the States of Jersey had begun a series of public works of their own, substantially reducing the labour pool and few locals worked for the new masters despite the lure of high wages and better rations.

However the Germans did find a ready pool of labour amongst those Irishmen who, neutrals, had been caught in Jersey by the rapidity of the invasion.

In June 1941 Hitler had ordered the invasion of Russia and in the spring of 1942 the first Russian and Polish prisoners of war arrived to swell the ranks of the forced labourers.

Having been marched right across Europe they were in a pitiful condition. Worse, being Slavs, the Germans regarded them as untermenschen, literally sub-humans, and treated them worse than domestic animals, slaves to be worked to death. In no time at all Jersey was hosting many thousands of these unfortunates as the occupiers embarked upon their defensive projects which would involve the removal of a staggering 244,000 cubic metres of rock. To put this into a wider context, the entire length of the Atlantic Wall (from Norway to the Pyrenees) involved the removal of just 11,000 cubic metres more!

The German defensive plan was simple. Ring the islands with impregnable bunkers and seawalls and create a network of deep tunnels into which the entire garrison could descend in the event of an invasion. Just how effective this 'underground' concept was would be discovered at enormous cost in Allied lives at Monte Cassino, St Malo, Cherbourg, Caen and dozens of other strongpoints in Europe as the defences of the Third Reich crumbled.

In Jersey sixteen deep tunnels were planned, large enough to house the entire garrison (circa 15,000 men and less than 100 women), their guns, ammunition, vehicles, fuel and food. They were described as Höhlgangsanlagen or 'cave shelters' and were all to be deep enough to survive intense bombing and shellfire. In World War I, bunkers just 40 feet deep survived the artillery barrage that preceded the Battle of the Somme, the greatest barrage of all time. The average depth of the tunnels in Jersey was more than 100 feet.

Of these, less than half were actually usable by the time the OT labourers were withdrawn early in 1944 and one was to become what is known today as the Jersey War Tunnels but for many years as the German Underground Hospital, the transition from artillery store and barracks to casualty clearing station being commenced in January 1944 (the conversion being carried out by Italian POWs who were no longer Germany's allies) when an Allied invasion of Europe became more than a distant possibility.

In the space of two years the occupiers and their reluctant workforce had turned thousands of tonnes of reinforced concrete into fifty-nine infantry and naval coastal defence strongpoints and bunkers with another thirty-one inland to provide a second line of defence.

Eleven tall towers for ranging and directing the sea-defence guns were planned on prominent headlands around the Island (although only three - at Noirmont, Corbière and Grosnez - were actually completed) and seven massive blockhouses designed to be regimental and battalion command posts (Kernwerken) were built amongst the fields and farms in St Peter in what is now The Living Legend Jersey Village.

Miles of coiled barbed wire were strung around the harbours, beaches and defence installations and 67,000 mines were sown. Sea walls were built and large tracts of the low lying and hence vulnerable west coast were flooded to create a watery trap for any invader.

The German chiefs of staff in Berlin were alarmed at the profligate waste of resources but no-one dare defy Hitler's instructions based on his belief that sovereignty in perpetuity of Britain's oldest possessions constituted an on-going major propaganda benefit.

As the occupation itself wore on and restrictions - such as the banning of radios - became tighter and tighter and foodstuffs bought by buying commissions in France became less and less nourishing, Islanders began to manifest their objection to occupation in different ways. V-signs scrawled in tar appeared on walls, telephone wires laid between military installations were cut and military vehicles were found to have all sorts of strange substances in their fuel tanks.

Dire punishments were promised for the perpetrators, including a well-publicised warning that 'saboteurs would be shot'. One Islander actually escaped by boat to Britain and the German headquarters in Paris initially retaliated by allowing no-one within ten kilometres of the coast. Except there is nowhere in the Islands that is not within ten kilometres of the coast! However the Geheimefeldpolizei were assiduous in hunting down 'saboteurs' and many Islanders found themselves incarcerated in their own Public Prison or, much worse, condemned by a military court to be sent to France and, in a number of unfortunate instances, to horrific imprisonment and death in concentration camps. In September 1942 it was announced that Jersey residents born in England, and their families, would be evacuated to Germany in retaliation, it is understood at Hitler's personal insistence, for similar deportations of German civilians from Persia (now Iran). In all, 1,200 men, women and children from Jersey, 825 from Guernsey and 11 from Sark were deported to internment camps at Laufen, Bad Wurzach and Biberach in southern Germany. The German authorities in the islands resisted complying with this order for as long as possible (for partly humanitarian but mostly logistic reasons) since the original order from Germany had been received the year before. Thousands of Islanders turned out to see the unfortunates off at the quayside and four youths - Frank Le Pennec, Hugh La Cloche, Frank Killer and Joe Miére - sang "There always be an England" so lustily that they were arrested and given a beating by the naval police for their patriotic fervour.

Early in 1943 those with concealed radios could tell their friends that the tide of war was gradually changing. Where there had only been German victories there were now only defeats. In January General Montgomery's Eighth Army, the Deserts Rats, began, at El Alamein, the mighty push that would eventually drive the Germans out of North Africa. In February an entire German Army of more than a quarter of a million men surrendered at Stalingrad.

By May 1943, British and American forces were fighting their way up Italy and on 4 June, the US Fifth Army took Rome and by mid-September Benito Mussolini, the Italian dictator, had been deposed and Italy surrendered unconditionally.

Despite the reverses, the German forces in Jersey continued their building programme unabated. By January 1944, 1,555 acres of Jersey's rich arable land had been lost to military constructions leaving the island littered with building materials, often disused railway tracks and stark edifices in concrete and steel. Because of the reduction in the usable land for growing foodstuffs, it was suggested that all private lawns be dug up and planted. The Jersey cow, a pure breed for more than two hundred years, came under threat as other breeds were imported to boost milk and beef production. Fortunately Jersey's farmers, jealous of the Jersey's uniqueness, kept the breeds well apart. Animals had to be registered with the German authorities but since it was almost always only the farmer who was present when his cows or pigs gave birth, the numbers given to the inspectors were often fictitious and sooner or later roast beef, veal or pork would make a welcome appearance in the family's diet.

Nevertheless early in 1944, the OT workforce began to be withdrawn to work on the defences of mainland Europe. The German High Command was convinced that an Allied invasion of Europe would come some time that year. Adolf Hitler was convinced that the Allies would invade in the region of the Pas de Calais because of its proximity to the English coast but General Erich Marcks, the commander-in-chief of the German forces in north-western France, predicted accurately that the invasion, when it came, would occur on the wide beaches of Normandy. His view was supported by Field Marshal Erwin Rommel who sought to retain much of the workforce to reinforce the defences of Normandy against Hitler's determination to fortify the Pas de Calais. No more than 200 OT workers remained in Jersey, their numbers boosted by Italian prisoners of war, as the garrison steeled itself for invasion. Would the Allies use the Islands as practice for the real thing or as stepping stones into mainland Europe?

The garrison practised their anti-invasion strategies over and over again, expending thousands of rounds of ammunition and causing much annoyance to local residents as they were evacuated from coastal areas time and time again and suffered hailstorms of shrapnel that rattled on their rooftops and broke their windows.

Early in June 1944 Channel Islanders knew that at last something momentous was afoot. Throughout the night of 5/6 June they heard the drone of aircraft overhead and the unfamiliar sound of anti-aircraft fire in anger. The next morning the BBC announced that the D-Day landings in Normandy had taken place precisely where General Marcks had predicted. His judgement was vindicated although he himself was killed in an air strike on his headquarters just a few days later.

Initial euphoria at an early liberation for the Islanders soon dissipated. The Allies' struggle for Normandy and Brittany would take many weeks and no-one appeared to be giving the beleaguered Channel Islands a second glance. What's more, with the adjacent French coast soon in Allied hands, no more fuel, food or medical supplies could be imported from France.

In October, faced with a bleak and hungry winter, the Bailiffs of both Islands appealed to the International Red Cross for help. At first the British Government blocked the appeal. Food supplies would simply prolong the Germans' will to resist, they maintained, and, indeed, overtures to the German commander to surrender now that the Islands were isolated were curtly rebuffed. However, if the Germans were to be starved out then surely the Islanders would starve with them.

Fortunately, as hunger and the onset of winter exerted their iron grip, more sympathetic views eventually prevailed and at the year's end the Swedish cargo vessel Vega sailed to the Islands from Lisbon loaded with more than 750 tonnes of New Zealand and Canadian Red Cross prisoner-of-war parcels (and 13 million cigarettes!). The ship arrived in Guernsey on

Boxing Day and in Jersey on 30 December 1944 and the parcels were distributed immediately.

Thereafter the ship made monthly trips to the Islands to bring foodstuffs and such luxuries as flour (the local stocks being completely exhausted), soap and babies' nappies.

The Germans did not touch the Red Cross parcels but, with the civilian population now being fed, requisitioned anything else even remotely edible and despite Islanders keeping their dogs and cats under lock and key as best they could, many family pets ended up in the cooking pot.

Despite the advances of the Allies into Germany itself the first three months of 1945 brought no quick end to the siege and the newly appointed German commander in chief, Vizeadmiral zur See Friedrich Hüffmeier, told Bailiff Coutanche in February: "We will never surrender even if, at the end, you and I are eating grass."

In March the Germans mounted a raid on Granville on the nearby French coast hoping to capture supplies destined for the Allied armies who were now on the Rhine. Unluckily for the Germans, although their raid took the American garrison completely by surprise, they had miscalculated the tides and the vessels they had intended capturing were firmly seated on the mud of Granville harbour. Their only trophy was an English coaster carrying a few tonnes of bunker coal and scrap iron which was of little use to a garrison that already possessed thousands of tonnes of it. However, despite this setback, the Germans' show of aggression suggested their inevitable surrender was still a long way off.

On 8 May 1945 Winston Churchill broadcast from London that, as from the previous midnight, Germany had unconditionally surrendered, the ceasefire had taken effect all along the front and that 'our dear Channel Islands are also to be freed today…'

The broadcast was conveyed over loudspeakers to delirious crowds in Jersey's Royal Square but the reality was slightly different. The German forces, hungry but still at full strength and fully armed, were under the command of a single-minded naval officer who would only surrender if ordered to by his own superiors. Winston Churchill might say that 'our dear Channel Islands are to be freed today' but Friedrich Hüffmeier was still in charge and did not agree. He wanted an armistice, apparently believing that the civilian population under his control gave him a significant bargaining counter.

Thus, when the Royal Navy destroyer HMS Bulldog arrived off Guernsey expecting an unconditional German surrender, Hüffmeier's representative, Kapitanleutnant Armin Zimmerman (who still gave the Nazi salute when boarding the ship), suggested that the destroyer sail away while negotiations took place since the presence of a British warship so close to the Islands was "a provocative act".

The captain of Bulldog, aware of the dozens of heavy guns pointed in his direction, wisely complied to give time for the Germans to contact Berlin whence they were advised by the new German chancellor and their own commander-in-chief, Grossadmiral zur See Karl Dönitz, that Germany had indeed surrendered unconditionally and that they should now do the same.

Thus, at 7.14 am on Wednesday 9 May 1945, the day after the rest of Europe except for a number of other ports in France also under German naval command, the German forces in the Channel Islands surrendered without condition. Later that same day a British relief force (Force 135) finally arrived in the Islands amid heart-felt cheering, flag-waving and welcoming kisses. A five year nightmare was over and the Islands were free again.

However, as in France and the other occupied countries, following the exhilaration and happiness were darker, more violent, emotions.

Known black marketeers and those who been too friendly or co-operative with the occupiers came in for denunciation, abuse and even physical violence. Local girls who had consorted with the Germans (estimates of as many as 900 births to local girls and German fathers are a gross exaggeration, the true number being nearer a tenth of that) were branded 'Jerrybags'. Some had their heads shaved and one was thrown in the harbour while another, the once-flamboyant mistress of a high-ranking German officer, was doused in diesel oil. She was rescued by the police before her 'punishment' could be taken any further. One notorious collaborator surrendered herself with her daughter to the authorities and was locked up in the Public Prison from which hundreds of her fellow-Islanders had just been released. The Gfp personnel, also fearing reprisals, turned up at the Public Prison asking to be locked up for their own protection.

However reprisals against German personnel were almost non-existent and by mid-May the bulk of the occupiers, still numbering more than 12,000 men and a few women, were transferred in American tank landing ships to prison camps in Britain while 200 sappers remained to assist British bomb disposal experts in tracing the 67,000 mines that had been laid down.

Following the British soldiers and the American sailors who made up the liberating force, came an army of Whitehall 'warriors' to assess the damage done by the occupiers and to instigate measures for restoring the Islands' commerce and everyday life. The only currency in use was the German reichsmark and, in an outright gift of £7 million, these were redeemed by the British Exchequer at face value. Unfortunately, for them, many islanders failed to exploit the situation and one farmer, offered two suitcases full of reichmarks by a German officer just before the Liberation, promptly burnt them!

Many who had evacuated in 1940 returned from their exile as strangers, their children speaking in the strange accents of London, Bolton, Liverpool and Glasgow. Young men in demob suits returned from the services, sometimes to find pre-war girlfriends still waiting for them but, as often, that the girls had married someone else.

Deportees also returned but there were many gaps in their ranks. A few, a very, very few, returned from imprisonment in Germany's horrific concentration camps, among them school-teacher Harold Le Druillenec, imprisoned for concealing a radio set, and the only British survivor of notorious Belsen. However his sister, Louisa, imprisoned for harbouring an escaped Russian slave worker, had died in the gas chamber at Ravensbrück.

In later years some commentators would remark on a lack of organised resistance and even active co-operation with the occupiers. What they forgot is that unlike most of the occupied countries of Europe where there were several hundred of the occupied to every single occupier, in the Channel Islands that ratio was never less than one to three. Also there was no maquis or mountains in which to hide. When asked how he resisted, war-time Bailiff Alexander Coutanche maintained that he 'protested' and kept on protesting. Other, more overt, resistance would have been futile.

However a group, which included several avowed local Communists, did try, towards the end of the Occupation, to foment mutiny amongst the garrison who were increasingly worried by the situation at home as the Allied bombing campaign pulverised Germany's cities. They managed to destroy a store at the main German bakery with stolen explosives but the Germans were well aware of the attempted coup (having been kept informed by one of the group's members) and did nothing to stop it other than to ensure that there was nothing in the store worth blowing up!

Their reasoning was that were they to report the existence of saboteurs and Communists in the Island, the Nazi Sicherheitsdienst, the infamous security service, would have involved itself in the Islands' affairs and the German military authorities did not want that any more than the Islanders would have done.

Nevertheless Islanders did resist, some methodically, some with almost careless disregard for their lives.

Acts of rebellion and sabotage, printing and distributing news sheets from the BBC broadcasts, concealing radios, harbouring escaped forced labourers and slave workers, were commonplace and subject to savage reprisal if the perpetrators were caught. By the end of the Occupation more than two and a half thousand Islanders had served time in the local Public Prison for activities against the occupiers and the prison was so full that there was a waiting list for cells of those under sentence.

Nevertheless, throughout the Occupation, only one person was shot by firing squad in the Islands (although the Germans did execute a number of their own personnel for military offences) and this was a paroled French soldier who, with a number of comrades, had fled from France and, landing in Guernsey, believed that a landfall had been made in Britain. Since breaking parole was an offence all sides recognised, despite the severity of the penalty imposed on the group's leader, no action was taken against the perpetrators of the penalty after the Liberation.

After the adjacent coast of France came under Allied domination in mid-1944, many Islanders escaped at risk of their lives, not just from the fourteen miles of fickle tides and currents, but also because the German coastal patrols tended to shoot first and ask questions afterwards. Although the shore patrols tended to aim at the boats rather than their occupants, many would-be escapers drowned when their bullet-ridden craft sank beneath them.

Although it was unknown for the German authorities to take and punish hostages in the Channel Islands (although they threatened to do so on many occasions), the number of Islanders, non-combatant civilians, who were imprisoned, suffered and died during the five years of enemy occupation is a tribute to the courage and rugged, obstinate individualism that the people of the Islands have shown for a thousand years of proud, and still undefeated, independence.

A couple of German troops outside St Helier Town Hall in 1944
CIP Collection

THE FLAGS

Every year, on 26 June, Mr Doug Ford from Jersey Heritage will hoist flags on the signal mast at Fort Regent from dawn until sunset to commemorate the return of the first ship bringing evacuees back to their beloved Island of Jersey.

The vessel that returned home with the first 1000 evacuees was the Southern Railways steamer 'Isle of Guernsey', still in her grey wartime livery, and commanded by Jerseyman Capt. H. F. Breuilly with Jerseyman Capt. Bernard Picot as his Chief Officer.

On that day the flags signalled the words "Home Again", which must have meant a lot to all the evacuees returning to Jersey and also to the families and friends that had gathered to welcome them at the Albert Pier.

This must have been such a fantastic occasion with the sounds of cheers, people waving banners and flags and many tears of happiness.

It will certainly be a day to remember and one that has gone down in Jersey's history.

Jean McLaughlin

The Flags on the signal mast. Photograph reproduced by kind permission of
Graeme Delanoe

213

PLAQUES AT THE ALBERT PIER

Most of the 5,000 people of Jersey who left the Island in 1940, departed from St Helier on the New North Quay and the Albert Pier.

To commemorate this important departure I arranged for two plaques to be placed on the wall opposite the Royal National Lifeboat Institution station on the Albert Quay. These were constructed by Mr Mark Reynolds from monumental masons F J Carter Limited.

The money raised to buy these plaques was donated by the evacuees of Jersey, after I spoke of my intentions on BBC Jersey. The Jersey Evening Post also wrote an article on the subject.

The late Brigadier Terry Troy unveiled the plaque commemorating those who joined the Forces and he also worded the inscription on the plaque. I am truly grateful to Brigadier Troy for his dedicated help as we worked together as a team.

Two gentlemen unveiled the plaque commemorating the evacuees of Jersey. Harold John Noel, who at the time of the unveiling was ninety years old and thus one of the oldest living evacuees, and Maurice Le Cocq, who was the youngest evacuee having left at the age of six weeks with his parents, brothers and sisters. These gentlemen and the Brigadier felt very honoured and privileged to unveil the Jersey flag-draped plaques sixty one years after the events they commemorated.

This Ceremony took place on Sunday 15 September 2006 in the presence of his Excellency the Lt Governor Lt General Sir Andrew Ridgway and Lady Ridgway and Deputy Bailiff Mr Michael Birt and Mrs Birt. Mr Birt is now the Bailiff of Jersey and our Patron. Also present was the Constable of St Helier Mr Simon Crowcroft who is also a patron while Mrs Caroline Routier, a teacher at First Tower School, was present with some children who dressed in war time clothing to reflect the era.

The Very Reverend Robert Key, Dean of Jersey, and Father Don Clement conducted the very moving ceremony and blessed the plaques.

We also had two flag bearers from the Royal British Legion, Mr Laurie Mould and Mr Nigel Le Monnier, music from the Caledonian Pipers led by Mr Jimmy McGovern and a bugler played the Last Post. Finally there was Mr Graeme Delanoe from the Jersey Military Vehicle Club.

This was a very special and important ceremony for the evacuees of Jersey and the people who attended. This will never be forgotten and will always be in our memories and mark a special day in Jersey history. We will never be forgotten again.

Permission was granted in 2009 by Harbour Master Capt. Howard Le Cornu and Jersey Harbours' commercial director Mrs Myra Shacklady for lights to be placed above the plaques and these will now be lit for ever more.

Jean McLaughlin

School children from First Tower School dressed in war time clothing to reflect the era.

Photographs reproduced by kind permission of Graeme Delanoe

THE VESSELS WHICH TOOK PART IN THE EVACUATION OF JERSEY

20 June 1940

Archangel	*Antiquity*	*Autocarrier*
Broomfield	*The Baron*	*Coral*
Hoddere	*Malines*	*Nagtira*
Perelle	*Porthmorna*	*St Bedan*
Seaville	*Suffolk Coast*	*Stork*
West Coaster		

21 June 1940

Atlantic	*Brittany*	*Carabin*
Dominium	*Felspar*	*Fintain*
Gorecht	*Hindsrig*	*Isle of Sark*
Maidstone	*Ringwood*	*Vega*
Shepperton Ferry	*Whitstable*	

Many of these vessels had a gross tonnage of under 1,000 tons and most were general cargo vessels although several usually carried coal and fertilizer. Shepperton Ferry was a passenger and train ferry that usually operated from Harwich to the Hook of Holland while Isle of Sark and Brittany were both Southern Railway passenger steamships. Ringwood and

Whitstable were cargo vessels operated by the Southern Railway with usual accommodation for 12 passengers. Isle of Sark was the last vessel to leave Jersey on 28 June. While in Guernsey later that same day she was subjected to attack by the Luftwaffe. She left that evening under the cover of darkness for Southampton. Despite the very imminent threat of German invasion (they invaded the following day) she carried only 400 passengers, a thousand less than her capacity.

Principal source : Occupation F2.7 Société Jersiaise

Dressed overall, Captain Breully brings Isle of Guernsey through St Helier pier heads 26 June 1945

Isle of Guernsey with Captain Breully in command was the first mailboat to arrive in St Helier after the Occupation. She arrived on 26 June 1945 still in her wartime colours. I believe he was also master when she made her last ever sailing from Jersey to Weymouth on 10 June 1961. Sadly, Captain Breully died at his home in Hampshire the following month and, at his request, his ashes were scattered in the sea off La Corbière on 25 July 1961 from the cargo vessel Moose commanded by his former first officer, and fellow Islander, Captain Bernard Picot.

Friends of the Maritime Museum

LIGHTER MOMENTS DURING THE EVACUATIONS

A Leap of Faith

One young man, on arriving at the harbour and seeing that the gangway was about to be lifted away, took a flying leap and landed on the deck exactly as the moorings were being cast off.

Tea or Coffee for General de Gaulle?

On Monday, 17 June 1940, a small aircraft flew unescorted up the west coast of France. On board was General Edward Spears, military liaison officer to Prime Minister Winston Churchill, and with him was 49 years old Brigadier-General Charles de Gaulle, who, until the day before had been France's Deputy Defence Minister.

Spears and de Gaulle were on their way from Bordeaux to London where the gawky general would become the leader of the Free French. Despite being warmly welcomed by Churchill (although he would have preferred to have greeted former Premier Paul Reynaud or Interior Minister Georges Mandel) Charles de Gaulle was very soon standing on his dignity which, from that day forth, became the wounded dignity of France.

The aircraft needed to refuel and landed at Jersey Airport. Generals Spears and de Gaulle repaired to the nearby Alexandra Hotel (today the St Peter's Country Inn) where de Gaulle, having been entrusted with 100,000 francs by Premier Reynaud, invested in a case of Scotch whisky. However, the restaurant being closed, all that could be offered by way of refreshment was a cup of coffee. Later de Gaulle would confide to his diary that he did not know what it was he had been offered and assumed it was tea! In all likelihood it was a concoction popular in Britain at the time (long before British taste buds became acclimatised to the real thing) whereby liquefied coffee essence was mixed with chicory and topped up with hot water and milk.

His brief visit is commemorated in a plaque at Jersey Airport and also a Cross of Lorraine in a St Helier park. Within a matter of weeks the Alexandra Hotel had been taken over by Maschinengewehr-Bataillon 16 (Machine Gun Battalion 16) as its headquarters with an array of anti-aircraft guns on the roof.

(Reprinted from 'We Shall Eat Grass' by Peter Tabb)

"Has your missus been evacuated?"

"Not yet, but she's takin' all sorts of pills!"